A World Elsewhere: The New American Foreign Policy

The Rules of the Game

Solvency: The Price of Survival. An Essay on American Foreign Policy

(editor) *Crisis in the Middle East*

(editor) *Atlantis Lost: U.S.-European Relations After the Cold War*
(with Earl C. Ravenal)

Solvency:
The Price of Survival

James Chace

SOLVENCY: THE PRICE OF SURVIVAL

An Essay on American Foreign Policy

Random House New York

Library of Congress Cataloging in Publication Data

Chace, James.
Solvency, the price of survival.

1. United States—Foreign policy—1977–
I. Title.
JX1417.C45   327.73   80-6005
ISBN 0-394-50754-1

Manufactured in the United States of America
2 4 6 8 9 7 5 3
First Edition

FOR SUSAN

Acknowledgments

IN THE CONCEPTION and execution of this work, I owe a special debt of gratitude to Jason Epstein, whose wisdom sustained me every step of the way.

I am deeply gratified for the thoughtful counsel I have received on the manuscript from William P. Bundy, Anton de Porte, David Fromkin, David Ives, Nicholas X. Rizopoulos, Robert Silvers, Helena Stalson and John Watts. For their helpful views on aspects of a work in progress, I also thank Ann Crittenden, Lucy Despard, Robert Legvold and Michael Lemmon. For her calm and helpful presence, I am particularly beholden to Mae Benett. Mark Gauthier has also been of notable help and support in completing this manuscript. And I owe Grace Darling more than I can express for her continuing encouragement of my work throughout the years.

I have profited enormously during the writing of this book by attending two seminar series at The Lehrman Institute—one organized by David P. Calleo on American foreign economic policy in the 1960s and 1970s, and the other by Robert W. Tucker on U.S. national security.

Most important of all, I want to thank Susan Chace, my wife, for her telling insights into the meaning of this book and her grace throughout the writing of it.

Contents

Solvency:
The Price of Survival

I

BECOMING INSOLVENT

A T TIMES I think I live in a ruined city. Here, some are protected and some are not. Those like me, who seem safe, have sought out apartments and houses like barracks. Safe from bad surprises. The lines of demarcation between "us" and "them" are drawn, as they have always been, but they are no longer clear. We had to be taught where the lines begin and end and how to maneuver alongside them. Now we are always alert, wired, so to speak, against trouble.

Statistics that show more crime a century or so ago than today distort the way we live now. Violence has grown random since the war, and we are all on our guard. No longer are there nineteenth-century ghettos like Hell's Kitchen, where an outsider could choose to enter or not at his peril.

Then the risk was real and known. Now trouble can come from anywhere. Not just physical assault. Most of us—if the means, however modest, are available—have found ways of coping with that. What seems to have happened is that society at large, both at home and abroad, has grown disorderly. In searching for some kind of order that goes beyond the self, I am haunted by the possibility of a world where laws are not obeyed, where the state is predatory or disintegrating, where terrorism has replaced large-scale warfare and the balance of power among nations has broken down with nothing to replace it.

In the South Bronx, less than a fifteen-minute drive from where I live on Central Park West in Manhattan, the buildings are burned out and still burning for miles on end. Just yesterday, I saw an old man carrying blackened logs to a fire he was feeding on a street corner. Nearby, Christmas ornaments hung from a chain-fence bazaar. In front of the fence, there is a newspaper stand. The bold headlines read: "Iran Terrorists Slay American." Beyond the auto hulks, the Garden of Eden Pentecostal Church blossoms like a floating island.

Is it just a question of "the metropolis"? Should we then abandon it and try to find the civic virtues of the community in smaller cities? Should I?

Not so long ago, I returned to the place where I was born and reared, the Massachusetts mill town of Fall River, which I remembered as comprehensible, but bleak and without promise. Because the collapse of the textile industry had come a full ten years before the Great Depression of the 1930s, the city of about 100,000 had long suffered from an endemic form of despair. Irresponsibility on the part of the mill barons, who reaped large profits during the boom years of World War I but who put nothing aside for capital improvements, combined with the overweening demands of the unions, helped quickly drive the textile industry south where, after all, the cotton grew.

I remember reciting the numbers as a schoolboy: in 1875, with 42 mills, Fall River was the largest cotton-manufacturing city in America; in 1911, it surpassed Manchester, England as the greatest cotton-spinning city in the world; in 1929, there were 101 textile mills; in 1940, 28 textile mills. Today, none. The mill buildings are therefore changed after thirty years. They no longer contain looms that weave cotton cloth, and from the outside, at least, they no longer seem the dark, satanic emblems of the industrial revolution, but rather antique, ivied-over. They have become romantic ruins.

Where I grew up the streets were not mean or hostile; but as you passed the city hall toward the south end, known as the Globe, the streets were ravaged by potholes and garbage. As in the other mill towns of Massachusetts, these ghettos built for the cotton workers always seemed built after the ugliest design that could be devised—blue and pink and brown tenements that sagged against one another. It was as though the cultivated New England landscape had been punished for its luck—the taste of the Georgian and Federal periods—that made possible elsewhere those village greens with their Puritan-white churches and shingled cottages.

Now, a generation later, the exteriors of the three- and four-story tenements are deceiving. There are no gaping

5

windows, no pocked walls, no graffiti; even the pillars sup-
porting the tiers of porches seem not to buckle severely.
Since the outsides are rarely painted but are, rather, covered
over by a colored sandpaper-like asphalt shingle, the deterioration doesn't seem so marked. But the decay is there even
so: the hallways bare of plaster, outhouses in the back, cold-
water flats, walls stripped bare. Outside one such neighborhood there is a small park. It was empty, swings broken,
cement cracked in a hundred places. The baseball batting
cage had long since been torn down. Trees that had once
lined the streets had somehow disappeared—ripped by the
hurricane of 1944 and never replaced, or withered by dis-
ease. A former high city official said to me without joy or
sadness: "We should let Fall River fall into ruin and build
a new city in the country." What happened to Fall River—
the abuse of capital, the failure to maintain productivity, the
price of labor, the flight of industry—should have been a
warning to the country at large, but it went unheeded.

Back in New York six of us gather for dinner. The apart-
ment is well appointed. Even the most casual pieces have
been chosen with care. The furnishings—the wine-red walls
in the dining room and the dusky bookcases behind the
piano draped with an embroidered cloth—all reflect the
European heritage of the owners. Their fathers had come to
America and sought their fortunes; their children, one an
anthropologist, the other a reporter, are articulate, conten-
tious, committed to those liberal, humane values that define
Western civilization. Even the masks from New Guinea
that hang from the ceiling derive from the pursuit of these
values commonly identified with freedom and self-fulfill-
ment. The room is closed in, a safe and private place.

Outside the snow has been falling and the dark spaces above the rooftops of the reconverted town houses are rimmed with white. Walking home after dinner, I buy a newspaper. The prediction is for five inches. If the report holds, the park will be filled with toboggans and sleds, and the eroded grass will be concealed, broken fences and broken bottles skinned over by healing snow. At this moment the park seems a repository of the common good—workable, usable, enhancing the life of the city. Or at least until the snow melts, and the neglected landscape is laid bare. The physical wrongdoing, so it seems, betrays a deeper disorder. It is the state itself, unable to respond to the demands made upon it, that like the late Roman metropole has lost all control over the "vast machine."[1]

WE ARE certainly a rich country. Our gross national product, as we enter the decade of the 1980s, is over a trillion dollars. We are told our standard of living is the highest among the great powers. Yet we can't afford a lot of things we once could and even those who are better off than their parents expect to be worse off in the future. The South Bronx was a functioning community when we were less rich. Most of us usually assume that the reason for this is that nowadays we use the money for something else. But if so, for what? There are those who would answer that question by citing the military budget running at well over $100 billion a year. The Carter administration was even prepared in 1980 to consider spending $30 billion on a new system of movable MX missiles as part of a continuing arms race with the Soviet Union. Yet, with all this expenditure, we are hard put to maintain a large standing army in Europe, and, in the parlance of military planners, we are prepared to fight only one and one-half wars—a doubtful figure, at best. In the early 1960s, however, we not only kept up a large army in Europe but claimed we were able to fight two and one-half wars. Our commitments have not significantly lessened, yet we are supposed to support about the same degree of potential involvement with smaller conventional forces.[2]

Then is the money going for public services? Evidently not. In New York and in other cities garbage is collected spasmodically, the police are undermanned and neighborhoods unsafe. Subways are such an assault on the senses that to descend into one seems a punishment. And even the best of our railroads are hard put to maintain their roadbeds, their schedules, their coaches, their debt service.

If the public services are in decay and the conventional military forces reduced to the degree that many believe may be inadequate for our national security, then maybe the answer is to levy greater taxes on the people. But the tax burden is already so severe that American citizens are reluctant to bear greater taxes for new schools, for better health care, for improving the quality of the very life they deplore.

How, then, did we get into this messy state? Felix Rohatyn, who was instrumental in devising ways of preventing New York City from going bankrupt in the mid-1970s, compares America now to New York then. "Like New York," he says, "America finds herself with increasing debts, both internal and external. In seeking to pay off debts, New York relied on short-term notes, the United States printed money. They neglected capital formation in other areas. Thus, when physical plants began to deteriorate, there was no financial plan already thought out to maintain or improve them. There was no financial plan either to cover greater and greater liabilities incurred by private and public pensions or social security. And jobs in the private sector were driven out by high taxes and low productivity."[3]

One of the ways out of this dilemma other than reduced consumption of television sets, electric typewriters and Adidas running shoes—what we call our standard of living —would be to increase America's productivity. What this would mean is investing our income in new machinery, working harder and consuming less than we produce. To do this would require some personal sacrifice, and no one seems willing to curb his or her appetite for consumption when the rewards for such sacrifice appear random. But if we did increase our productivity, this would allow us to sell more and buy more—both at home and abroad. Instead, we are going in quite the opposite direction. Growth in productivity has gone down from an average rate per year of about three percent for the thirty years after World War II to about half that rate in the late 1970s. Business investment in the United States, as a share of our gross national product as we enter the 1980s, is already two-thirds the rate in West Germany, less than half the rate in Japan.

Moreover, throughout this decline in productivity we have been profligate. We have continued to buy abroad, most dramatically by increasing our imports of foreign oil, allowing them to rise a staggering forty-two percent between 1973 and 1978, until they ran to about fifty percent of our needs at the end of the decade. Partly as a result of our oil dependence, America's visible overseas trade, which was in surplus from 1893 to the 1970s, was running in 1978 at a deficit of about $30 billion a year, just about the amount initially estimated to build the MX missiles. To finance the deficit, the government simply created more credit—IOUs that become worth less and less to whoever holds them, as our deficits increase and we go on printing more money to cover them. We go on printing money and importing oil and running shoes because the alternative—to live within our diminished means—seems unthinkable. Thus, inflation becomes not an aberration within an otherwise healthy economy but the definition of the economy itself.

For a time, America's declining productivity and the consequent weakening of the dollar could be concealed by the fact that the dollar was the main currency used by all nations to settle their accounts among themselves. It was, in a sense, world money, and thus the United States could finance its external deficit by simply issuing more dollars. What General de Gaulle once called our "exorbitant privilege," however, became an enormous disadvantage when foreigners began to lose confidence in America's ability to manage her economy.[4] This meant that we had to pay more and more dollars for the goods *they* produced and we imported. They also paid less and less for the goods *we* produced and they imported. In short, when dollars were scarce overseas in the 1950s, foreign goods we imported were cheap because we held dollars that foreigners wanted; by the 1970s, when this dollar shortage no longer existed and indeed foreigners held more dollars than they wanted, our goods became cheaper for them. Rather than importing foreign goods at high prices, the American consumer should have been able to spend his money on cheaper domestic products, which would have reduced the flow of dollars abroad. However, domestic producers often simply raised their prices to compete with foreign imports that were taxed or otherwise restricted from entering the home market, thus aggravating inflation.

As we enter the 1980s, U.S. administrations, reacting to the passions of the electorate, remain reluctant to forgo printing money. To suggest otherwise would be to ask the voters to give up their privileged position to import whatever they want with an ever-devaluating currency. Yet, like it or not, we may be facing a long-term decline in our freedom to consume. With the dollar no longer so desirable as the key currency to provide liquidity or world money to finance global trade, a world of several key currency blocs is beginning to emerge that will share this function with the dollar. The Japanese yen and the German mark—and perhaps, in time, a European currency unit—already rival the dollar as favorable currencies to hold in reserve or to exchange for goods and services. The reason for holding such currencies is simply that people believe the economies that produce them are better managed than ours, and thus a holder of marks or yen gets more goods for his money than he would with dollars. Moreover, the size of the world economy has grown so great that the U.S. economy—even at its most powerful—is no longer able to underwrite all the world money needed for trade and investment.

If confidence in the American economy falls so low that investment in dollar-denominated securities is scorned except at very high interest rates, then America will find it even more costly to buy what it needs abroad—petroleum, for example. Already, the OPEC cartel of oil-producing nations, fearful that its dollar reserves will be worth less and less as inflation undermines the value of the dollar, has entered the decade by proposing to use a number of currencies as its reserves, and, finally, by buying gold as a last defense against the collapse of the Western economies.

As Rohaytn has pointed out, the forces that had earlier been driving New York City toward bankruptcy were doing the same to the United States, though literal bankruptcy is not really possible for America "since the Treasury can, and does, always print money." In reality "America's debts are continually stretched out, to be repaid in the future with currency worth less and less." This is what economists call inflation and what Rohaytn calls "a polite word for gradual bankruptcy." The question for America, then, is how to conform her rate of consumption to her diminished productivity before a collapse of confidence in the American economy results in a collapse of confidence not only in the international monetary system, but in the United States itself.

For there is no way to insulate the American economy from the world economy. To erect high barriers to protect our uncompetitive goods would most likely create a hostile world of retaliatory protectionist restrictions; to start a cycle of competitive devaluations among nations to gain export advantages or competitive interest rates to attract investors —both of which we have done—could produce beggar-thy-neighbor policies in the monetary and balance-of-payments fields. And for Washington to impose controls over foreign exchange transactions to conceal the effect of inflationary domestic policies would mean the end of the dollar's convertibility and leave those holding dollar reserves with currency that would lose its value to such a degree that the result would be international chaos. Even in 1980, the American economy is enormous—three and a half times as big as West Germany's—and, like a leviathan's, its collapse would help to pull down others around it.

A more optimistic projection, but a difficult one to attain, would be for Americans to produce more while at the same time accepting, at least temporarily, a reduced standard of living. During such a time, the public and private sectors would join together to rebuild America's industrial base and to upgrade her transportation system, to develop new sources of energy while consuming less, to increase basic research and development, to construct modern factories and provide them with the most efficient machinery that technology offers, with the high costs of American labor offset by greater efficiency leading to greater productivity. Such a program could lead to bigger exports, low inflation, a more stable dollar and, in the long term, a higher standard of living.

To rebuild America in this way or to accept gradual bankruptcy—these are the choices before us. But the political difficulties standing in the way of such rational choices are severe. It is hard indeed to imagine their being made at all until a great crisis is upon us—which it is—and is perceived as such—which it is not.

THE AMERICAN quandary of how to exert control over her own destiny at home is magnified by the fact that America's power to control events abroad has been sharply reduced.

For Americans who grew to maturity in the two decades after World War II, America's place in the international system was secure. Even the challenge from the Soviet Union seemed clear: the apparent necessity for America to maintain a worldwide military establishment was unquestioned, and the rich American economy was able to finance it.

Today, America, accustomed to behave in the postwar era as a nation whose economic and military resources granted her status as a superpower, unchallenged in the economic sphere even by her rival, Russia, lives in a strange new world. She finds herself in a situation where Russia is now roughly her military equal, or even her superior, with a global reach she did not possess even during the height of the cold war in the 1950s. What Russia has done—with an economy still far inferior to America's—is to concentrate her resources on building up her military might. The Soviet Union's strategic nuclear capacity has increased fivefold since 1964, and the buildup of its navy and air support facilities allows it to project power into distant areas, as its behavior in southern Africa has made evident. Each superpower now has more than enough strategic weapons to destroy the other many times over; but no longer does the United States possess absolute control of the air and sea as it once did. To reassert that preponderance—or even just to maintain strategic parity and restore a conventional rough balance of forces with the Russians—would further strain an economy that prefers consumption to investment.

The Soviet Union, on the other hand, runs a command economy, able to increase military spending at the expense of the consumer with no evident political costs. If the United States truly wants to compete with the U.S.S.R. on a military basis, we have the choice of either persuading our citizens to pay for these expenditures by increasing taxation and reducing spending in the public and/or private sector, or printing the money to provide both the military and the consumer goods we are accustomed to. This latter course is what Lyndon Johnson chose during the Vietnam War, a policy that helped bring on the high levels of inflation we have known since the late 1960s. It is a policy of asking for no important sacrifices—or, if there are any, they are generally imposed on the weakest elements of the society by cutting social services such as health and child care. For a still powerful but faltering economy such as ours, there are real costs to the cold war, and they should be borne by every sector of society.

Moreover, the cold war, which seemed about to end with the Nixon administration and its promise of détente that would ease Soviet-American relations, now appears to be revived. From the end of World War II to the end of the Vietnam War may soon be seen as simply phase one in a very long conflict. One might well ask, what were the stakes then? And what are they now? In the beginning, Russia and America, inheritors of the world leadership that Europe had lost, might have composed their differences and sought spheres of influence beyond Europe and the Western Hemisphere. Instead, the hostility that had existed since 1917 between the Western powers and the Soviet Union reasserted itself after the temporary wartime alliance against Nazi Germany.

In the view of American policy makers in the immediate postwar era, the role of the Soviet Union seemed likely to parallel Germany's behavior between the wars. The perception of the Soviet Union shared by most informed Americans during this period was of a Russia that refused to allow territories contiguous to her own—with the notable exception of Finland—to install governments that were anything but totally subservient to the dictates of Moscow. In short, though Washington was prepared to acquiesce in a Soviet sphere of influence in Eastern Europe, it was not prepared to accept Soviet military force in the area, denial of self-determination for the nations involved, and an apparent threat to Western Europe. A little over a decade after the war, however, the United States reluctantly accepted the partitioning of Europe, and erected a defense of Western Europe to preserve the status quo.

Having codified the partition of Europe by the early 1970s through a series of agreements between Western Europe and the United States on the one side, and Eastern Europe and the Soviet Union on the other, the two superpowers might have opened up a new era of cooperation. President Nixon himself spoke of the end of the era of confrontation.

But the conflict did not stop. For by the late 1970s the cold war had entered a second phase. Soviet aid to Egypt at the outbreak of the 1973 October War, Soviet airlifting of Cuban troops during the 1975 Angolan Civil War, Soviet matériel and advisers sent to Ethiopia in its conflict with Somalia in the Horn of Africa, Soviet aid to South Yemen on the Persian Gulf, the Soviet invasion of Afghanistan—

all this appeared as a growing threat to America's vital resources in the Middle East, to her alliance structure in the Eastern Mediterranean, and to her commitments to Israel and Egypt. Zbigniew Brzezinski, Carter's national security adviser, referred to the area stretching from Afghanistan to Angola as an "arc of instability." That instability seemed to the Carter Administration to require American intervention —political, economic and, if necessary, military—to protect American interests and to contain what Brzezinski saw as "an increase of Soviet power" in the region.

More to the point, the program of the Soviet Union—and particularly of the Soviet navy—to project power all around the world created in the minds of many Americans the impression that the U.S.S.R. is out to dominate nations far beyond its now accepted sphere of influence. Even for those who do not believe that we are witnessing a form of crude Soviet expansionism that aims at control of territory and peoples, there is little doubt that Moscow's military build-up reflects an effort to make the U.S.S.R. a global power at least equal to, if not surpassing, the United States. In Soviet Foreign Minister Andrei Gromyko's words, "today no question of any significance in world relations can be decided without, or in defiance of, the Soviet Union." And as Soviet strength has increased, ours has grown relatively weaker.

With the invasion of Afghanistan, for example, the Soviet Union for the first time used military force on a massive scale outside what the West considered its sphere of influence in Eastern Europe. As Soviet specialist Seweryn Bialer described it, such a strategy demonstrated "a new degree of confidence, self-assertiveness and expansionism," as the

Soviets "carefully and deliberately" chose new means—direct military intervention—to pursue an old goal, "the extension of political power abroad." Soviet behavior in Afghanistan also showed that the Soviets may have abandoned certain assumptions seemingly fixed in Soviet thinking— "that the Soviet Union had much to gain from the cooperation with the West, and especially the United States, and much to fear from the United States should its behavior transgress certain unstated but well understood bounds."[5] No longer did the Soviets feel they had to keep in balance their need to prevent a drift toward dangerous confrontation with the United States and their desire for gains. They believed that the SALT II arms-control agreement was dead, that food and technology would not be forthcoming from Washington (though they would be from other nations, including America's closest allies), and that an America unwilling to put her domestic house in order was not likely to show the steadiness of purpose in foreign policy that would sustain her commitments to the world.

Insofar as the United States vacillates in relation to the Soviet Union, the alliance structure we have built up since World War II may come apart, as it has already begun to do, just as the inability of the government to sensibly manage its currency has resulted in a lack of confidence on the part of our allies in American economic leadership.

We Americans are beset by a double image of ourselves: as both powerful and inadequate. Yet it is more than an image. It is true. We are powerful beyond the measure of any other nation in history and, as time passes, we are becoming more ordinary, more like the others, subject to unaccustomed constraints. How to reconcile these two truths with each other and with what Walter Lippmann, over a generation ago, laid down as a fundamental principle of a wise foreign policy: that it be solvent? By this he meant bringing into balance, with a comfortable surplus of power in reserve, a nation's commitments—economic, political, military—and a nation's power. For well over a decade we have not done so. As a consequence, the central question for American foreign policy is how to manage our domestic and foreign affairs in order finally to bring about a solvent foreign policy, if indeed we can.

IT WAS NOT always so. As an American out of college arriving in Europe in the fall of 1953, I saw an American predominance that seemed to ensure peace and prosperity in the West. Along with my youth, I took American power for granted. Both seemed limitless. Far from living in an anarchic world, I believed I lived in an orderly one. America's power far exceeded anything Russia could pretend to. In Asia, what was perceived as Sino-Soviet expansion had already been stopped by American troops in Korea. If anything, the Korean War seemed to guarantee American predominance in the Pacific. It had been the turning point in an anti-Soviet alliance that now included not only the United States and our wartime European allies, but also our former enemies, Germany and Italy. From my point of view, as a young American encountering a still-impoverished Europe, it seemed as though the French in particular were pursuing a lost dream, a colonial empire already gone at the seams, while trying to maintain France as a world power.

Looking back I realize no one could have foreseen the consequences of events in 1954. In that year, France's Indochina War ended, but it turned out to be only the first phase in a much larger struggle, one that would propel America toward the limits of her moral and economic power and signal the end of the bipolar world of the superpowers. Meanwhile, a scarcely noticed, poorly executed uprising in Algeria in November 1954 would topple the French Republic and eventually put Algeria in the vanguard of those nations of the Third World demanding reparations from America and the other rich nations as a way of atoning for their past history of exploitation and control. And then, as the year closed, the French government set up a secret group within its atomic energy agency that would make France a nuclear power. It was a policy designed not only to restore French primacy in Europe but also to put France to this extent beyond U.S. control after Washington had refused to aid the French with nuclear weapons to lift the siege of Dien Bien Phu during the Indochina War.

But politics, in the beginning, was far from my mind. I had come to Paris to study Delacroix and Baudelaire, the relationship between art and literature, not between the state and the society of nations. In contrast with the political decay of the Fourth Republic, Paris itself flourished. The leaves fell slowly from the chestnut trees throughout the long, beautiful fall, when even a week before Christmas it still seemed like summer. I saw Beckett's first play produced in the cramped Théâtre de Babylone. Camus and Sartre published novels and plays and went at each other. At the Trocadéro, Gérard Philipe played Lorenzaccio and the Cid.

But soon it became impossible for me to remain indifferent to politics, as impossible as it would have been for a foreign student coming to America in 1968. Whether or not to go on fighting the seven-year war in Indochina divided neighbor from neighbor, while the government, uncertain of its goals, refused to negotiate with the Communists, reluctantly supported the military commanders and too often asserted its faltering strength by striking violently at those who criticized it. There were meetings, cells of militants who stood, so it seemed, against everything: against German rearmament . . . against the Socialists . . . against the Gaullists . . . against the Communists . . . and, especially, against the war in Indochina, which was to end only a few months later in the decisive siege of Dien Bien Phu, with dangerous consequences for the United States.

By winter, things fell apart: there were riots to protest the Indochina War. My fellow students and I first gathered in the courtyard of the university, then, bursting forth, were pursued by the cape-swinging gendarmes along the Boulevard Saint-Germain toward the National Assembly. The chant *"Navarre au poteau"*—the commanding general in Indochina, to the gallows—later became *"de Gaulle au pouvoir,"* the same syllabic rhythm that echoed from automobile horns four years later when de Gaulle was called upon to settle a war in Algeria. For myself, I seemed to be caught in a situation where I shared both in the commitment and in the danger without quite knowing, as a foreigner, where my responsibility lay.

When I left Paris soon after the conclusion of the July Geneva Conference providing for French disengagement from Indochina, I returned to America believing that while the French had acted as an anachronistic colonial power, Americans, the first modern anticolonialists, stood for self-determination for all peoples. But, as I came to understand during the next decade of the cold war in the midst of a period of post-colonial upheaval, Washington's definition of self-determination generally meant "free elections," and a continuing commitment to the ideological and economic norms of the West. Revolutions, however, have rarely been won by men who favored those values. Moreover, in assessing the effect new nations might have on the struggle between America and Russia, Washington determined that anti-Communist governments best ensured an orderly world. And to achieve such a world, American power—political, economic, military, and backed domestically by a broad anti-Communist consensus—provided at least the appearance of stability in the West and on the periphery of Asia. The containment of possible Communist expansion, first in Europe and in the Eastern Mediterranean, then on the Korean peninsula, seemed an accomplished fact.

But in 1954, with the Geneva accords ending the French phase of the Indochina War, the Eisenhower administration committed itself to a deeper involvement in the global containment of communism than the country had bargained for. Unable to accept the loss of Vietnam to the Communists under Ho Chi Minh, Secretary of State John Foster Dulles believed that the two-year hiatus before elections, scheduled throughout Vietnam in 1956, would give enough time for a nationalist, anti-Communist regime to install itself firmly in the South. Two aims of American policy followed hard upon this. One was to supplant the residual French military mission in South Vietnam. The other was to find a non-Communist nationalist, a search that was finally concluded when Ngo Dinh Diem became prime minister. Neither Diem nor Ho was disposed to settle on the basis of free elections whether Vietnam should be reunited, and, with elections off, North Vietnam reopened the civil war with full force. It would last almost twenty years.

What is clear is that neither Dulles nor Eisenhower seized Geneva as a way of writing Indochina off to the Communists, which Eisenhower, at least, had the political strength to have done. They did not believe that Indochina was simply the end game of French colonialism, as India was Britain's. For Dulles, the line to be drawn against Communist expansion in Southeast Asia was not at the borders of Thailand or the Indonesian archipelago. It was straight across Vietnam at the 17th parallel. The consequences of this were to involve the United States itself in a war which cost 56,000 American lives and 150 billion American dollars —and all this for an area whose actual strategic importance to the United States was negligible. Thus, a little over a decade after the Geneva Conference, American policies devised in 1954 not only resulted in the frustration of U.S. military power and the failure of American moral certainty, but also contributed mightily to the breakdown of American economic predominance.

OF ALL the consequences of the Vietnam War, one of the least noticed at the time, and yet one of the most permanent, was the damage done to the American economy.

Many of the lessons of the war could be unlearned or forgotten or were the wrong lessons to begin with, but the impact of the war on the dollar both at home and abroad was such that further disorder was inevitable. The United States spent tens of billions of dollars on the destruction of Southeast Asia in a war that clearly hindered the building of any new, innovative industrial base at home. Nor did Lyndon Johnson have the political courage to tax the American people to pay for the war. The Johnson administration expanded the social programs of the Great Society and the Federal Reserve provided the dollars to finance these commitments, setting off the devastating inflation that now plagues us. America as the creator of the world's principal reserve currency allowed herself to run up deficits abroad while foreigners had to go on accepting the increasingly worthless dollars with which we bought their goods. (One later response was OPEC's decision in the 1970s to raise oil prices, in part to keep abreast of the failing dollar.) In large part, America fought the Indochina War on credit, borrowing on other people's productivity, just as New York City financed itself by borrowing from local banks. The time would come when America's credit rating would suffer, just as New York's did, as foreigners found themselves submerged in a glut of debased dollars.

None of this was apparent in 1954. For just as the Geneva Conference seemed to signal an end to the Indochina War and at least a grudging American acquiescence in the manner of its ending, the admission of the Federal Republic of Germany in October as a rearmed state participating in NATO seemed the final element in a strong military alliance

backed by American economic power. The head of the
Organization for European Economic Cooperation described Western Europe's economy in 1954 as more satisfac-
tory than at any other time in history, something no one
could have anticipated five years earlier.[6]

When the Indochina War against the French began in
1946, the United States was still committed to an open
world economy, to a belief, for example, that Britain should
dismantle its closed imperial markets, which represented
discriminatory treatment in international commerce. Free
convertibility of currencies and free movement of capital—
these were the goals of liberal America. After all, what could
be better than a liberal world order where money was easily
convertible from one currency to another, and countries
were pleased to welcome one another's trade and investment?[7] Especially was this the received wisdom after the
experience of the interwar period when economic blocs
warred against one another, when protectionism flourished
and competitive devaluation was the rule—a world of beggar-thy-neighbor states that weakened those who would
soon face Nazi aggression. But such a liberal world was not
immediately attainable.

At the end of World War II Western Europe was too
poor to compete in the open marketplace. Though, ideologi-
cally, Washington never gave up on the idea of a liberal
world economy, it became evident that the idea had to be
shoved aside during the cruel winter of 1947 when free
convertibility of British sterling ignited the collapse of the
British pound as holders of sterling rushed to convert their
pounds into dollars. Because British reserves and invest-

ments had been wiped out during the war, the Americans had already granted a loan to get the British economy moving again. With the collapse of sterling in 1947, however, the dollars Britain had obtained rapidly drained away.

While never abandoning the notion that free trade would be good for the world in general and for America in particular—whose goods were desired by one and all—Washington decided that a new system was needed to allow the Europeans temporarily to set up high tariffs and other barriers to free trade. Only in this way could the Europeans—acting as a bloc—grow strong enough to buy American products. Then, in the course of time, the tariff walls would crumble and worldwide free trade would be revived. (By the 1960s this is what generally happened but with far stronger competition from Europe and Japan than most of us had ever imagined.) The Marshall Plan was to supply the money that would allow Europe to build up her economy, and, in so doing, to buy American imports. The dollar shortage was to be overcome by American aid and to this end the United States in the 1950s was willing to run—and the Europeans eager to accept—overall American balance-of-payments deficits, largely as a result of U.S. military expenditures abroad. The need for a strong Europe to resist a Communist threat—perceived as coming from the Soviet Union and from internal subversion—meant not only a North Atlantic Treaty Organization but American dollars to finance it. In any case, a growing American economy would, everyone assumed, make good these short-term deficits.

Europe gladly accepted, indeed clamored for, American military protection in exchange for the prospect of rapid

economic recovery,[8] especially since by the end of the war
the United States had most of the world's gold reserves—
$22.8 billion worth in 1950—more than enough for the
United States to back up its expanding currency.[9] Thus,
though the European central banks were able to buy gold at
$35 an ounce, there seemed little need to do so, and when
the European currencies became convertible into dollars in
1958, most Europeans were happy to hold their reserves in
dollars rather than cash them in for gold. After all, dollars
could be invested at decent interest rates, as gold could not,
and an expanding world economy—the economy of the
1950s—meant that dollars were the currency needed for
world trade and investment.

Slowly the so-called dollar gap closed, as the Europeans
earned more dollars from their exports and from U.S. military expenditures and investments abroad. The cost of providing a *pax Americana*, first in Europe and then in the Far
East, needed a strong American economy with wise investments in new industries to keep up our competitive edge,
and a population willing to moderate its consumption for
the sake of investing in its own future. Above all, we had to
make sure our military expenditures overseas did not impair
the growth and productivity of new industry necessary to
keep up our favorable trade balance and to maintain our
ability to compete in world markets.

Throughout the Eisenhower and Kennedy administrations, the management of the American economy seemed
sound, with a low inflation rate and a favorable balance of
trade. Our overall payments deficits were justified in the
light of the obligations we eagerly assumed by extending our

military protection over others. But in fact, as Professor David Calleo has pointed out, during the 1950s a lower American rate of capital investment was beginning to mean "the relative decline of productivity—a decline thought both to reflect and to encourage the growing propensity of American companies to invest abroad."[10] Investment abroad, after all, seemed a sensible way for business to take advantage of cheaper foreign labor and to leap over the tariff walls the Europeans had erected in order to restore their economies. However, the Kennedy administration saw these trends as linked to a now too protracted balance-of-payments problem. "While," as Calleo notes, "the U.S. payments deficits until the late fifties could be blamed on aid programs and trade and currency discrimination to help European and Japanese recovery, by 1960 the U.S. payments deficit was persisting despite a general return to convertibility and a sharp improvement in the American trade surplus."[11] Much of this deficit was the price we were paying to maintain our role as the world's policeman.

The Kennedy administration's answer to these problems was to try to strengthen the economy by encouraging domestic growth through stimulating our appetite for greater consumption. Growth, in turn, would lead to new investments at home and these new investments would then result in still further growth and so halt the decline in American productivity. Wage/price guidelines would prevent inflation and retain American competitiveness in world markets. Moreover, stimulating growth at home would lead to reduced investment abroad, since American capital would be given incentives to stay at home to fuel the expanding economy. In case anyone missed the point, outflows of U.S. capital were restricted—a break from the liberal world economic order the administration espoused. In consequence, our currency was supposed to grow stronger, since the dollar outflow for corporate investment abroad had been a key factor in America's balance of payments deficit. In short, as Calleo points out, "American capital would be thus strengthening productivity at home rather than bolstering competition abroad."[12]

Finally, there was to be a new emphasis on reducing tariffs on goods at home and abroad to restore the traditional American commitment to free trade. The active promotion of free trade was designed to keep the world market open for American exports, particularly agricultural exports, and so improve the falling U.S. trade balance and America's balance of payments position. (In the long run agricultural exports did contribute to helping a faltering foreign trade, but they were not enough, for by 1971 the United States suffered its first trade deficit in the twentieth century. Our imports that year exceeded exports by $2 billion, and this, two years before the drastic hike in OPEC oil prices.)

The Kennedy administration's foreign aspirations, however, were such that the U.S. balance of payments deficits were not overcome. Like its predecessor, the Kennedy administration saw the deficits as a result of America's global commitments to maintain the peace. For in the overall balance there were two political items that helped drain a potential surplus. One was the overseas military cost and the other was foreign aid. And while agreements with our allies to buy our military hardware and with our foreign aid often tied specifically to agreements to buy U.S. goods helped mitigate the consequences of our military and political commitments, the Kennedy administration had no intention of reducing such commitments. On the contrary, these problems were the foreign political counterpart of an American order that had created a monetary system dependent on the dollar as the predominant currency for world prosperity.[13] At the same time, the need to keep the American domestic economy moving required relatively low interest rates at home; thus still more American dollars flowed abroad where interest rates were higher.

While our foreign economic problems were worrisome to the Kennedy administration, those years were, nonetheless, a time of low inflation and high growth. By and large, the European countries continued to have confidence in the management of the dollar, though the French were most critical of America's role as the centerpiece of the international monetary system in which dollars were literally supposed to be as good as gold. On the one hand, dollars were still needed as a form of international money because an expanding world economy required the enormous liquidity provided by the dollar to finance it; confidence in the management of the great U.S. economy was still such that foreigners were willing to hold dollars rather than exchange them for gold, while the United States was only too ready to supply them. On the other hand, the very willingness of foreigners to hold dollars far in excess of the gold reserves the United States was compelled to hold in exchange for them set the stage for global inflation—as dollars continued to flow abroad—which threatened the breakdown of the international monetary system.

The United States was creating its own credit. At some point or other in the 1960s, there was not enough American gold (still pegged at $35 an ounce as it had been since 1934) to redeem all the dollars held by foreigners. But most foreigners continued to hold their overseas dollars because they still believed that the United States could redeem them through its own production potential. Even so, some of these so-called Eurodollars were being cashed in for gold, which resulted in a further depletion of the U.S. gold reserves. What we were doing was printing dollars to borrow against the promise of an expanding future, a future that by 1980 had not in fact materialized.[14]

Nonetheless, until the dramatic escalation of the Vietnam War in 1965, it seemed likely that the United States would be able to improve its trade position and its productivity, and to contain inflation, while maintaining low unemployment and high growth. Instead, the Johnson administration found that it was not possible, as it had been during the Korean War, for an expanding economy to pay for the cost of combat. L.B.J.'s program was to fight a war without inflicting economic pain, without, as it were, disturbing the promise of a consumer society. It was part of the same promise we had believed in when we preferred to invest abroad in order to provide ourselves with goods produced by cheap labor, rather than invest at home to keep our industrial plant modern. Even in 1966, when the Defense Department informed the President that the war would cost between five and ten billion dollars more than had been estimated, Johnson still refused to cut domestic spending or ask Congress for a tax increase, for this could have meant the end of his social welfare programs.

When the President finally requested a tax increase in August 1967, Congress, its members also concerned for their political futures, delayed it for almost a year while the deficit rose to $25 billion.[15] Thus, throughout this period, even though there was real growth—as the President was committed to a full employment budget—there were ominous shadows. Inflation grew, with the consumer price index increasing by 2.9 percent in 1967 and by 5.9 percent in 1969. Wages rose correspondingly—5.7 percent in 1967, 7 percent in 1969.[16] Most serious of all, the money created when the Federal Reserve Bank financed a large part of the growing deficit was not being invested in the domestic economy but in the wasteful war in Southeast Asia.

Observing these policies the Europeans reacted by increasing their reserves of gold as they lost confidence in America's ability to manage her economy, just as banks began charging New York City higher interest as the city's faltering economy began to weaken its tax base. In so doing, the Europeans deprived themselves of the world money they were trying to protect. Ironically, it was not so much the balance-of-payments deficits—at least the still-modest ones that occurred during the first few years of the Vietnam escalation—that bothered the Europeans, but the relative size of the domestic budget deficit, which revealed the unwillingness of the participants in the economy to pay for the public services they demanded.

What the deficit reflects is the amount the consumer and the government spend in excess of what the country earns through production of goods and services. Spending more than a society earns tends to create inflation and erode the value of the currency—including, of course, the billions of dollars the Europeans are holding. The switch to gold, the price of which was eventually to exceed $800 per ounce by the end of the 1970s, was one consequence.

As the domestic economy was swept forward on a wave of inflation, we also sold less abroad, and so our trade balance declined further. While 1964 had seen the highest trade surplus since 1947, by 1966 the surplus had fallen to half that level, and by 1971 we saw the first U.S. trade deficit since 1893.[17] Moreover imports, *not including* military expenditures, increased by 70 percent between 1965 and 1969, a rise in those four years equal to that of the preceding nine years, that is, from 1956 to 1965.[18] Thus, continuing to fight a war in Southeast Asia while maintaining a powerful military presence in North Asia and Europe—and all this in the face of declining productivity, continuing inflation, high labor costs and the expectation of a higher standard of living —how could the United States also preserve a strong dollar backed by gold? The answer was: It could not.

In 1971 President Richard Nixon announced that the United States was no longer willing to convert dollars into gold. Our indebtedness was such that we no longer possessed enough gold to back the dollars we had printed and sent abroad. Foreigners were now expected to go on using dollars as world money, even though there was no gold behind them; as their confidence in the management of the American economy declined, however, their willingness to hold dollars declined as well. They sought "harder" currencies, such as the West German mark or the Japanese yen, a tribute to German and Japanese productivity and low infla-

33

tion rates. The depreciation of the dollar on the foreign exchanges further fed domestic inflation as the cost in dollars of imported goods rose during the Ford and Carter administrations. Domestic manufacturers, far from underselling imports, took advantage of higher prices for competing exports to raise their own prices. With billions of dollars still held abroad, foreigners lived in fear that these would some day prove almost worthless.

By 1978, for the first time in memory, the United States faced a situation where the weakness of its currency on the world's exchanges affected the domestic life of its citizens. The Federal Reserve, in order to defend the value of the dollar abroad, raised interest rates at home, at the expense of American borrowers and business investment. But a year later, the U.S. rate of inflation, far from diminishing, grew worse. The dollar fell further and the Fed again raised interest rates, this time to unprecedented levels. These measures, and others designed to curb the expansion of domestic credit, managed to shore up the dollar temporarily, but as interest rates fell, which they did a few months later when the economy slid into a rapid recession, the dollar fell again on the world's exchanges. For the problems that have plagued the American economy since the Vietnam War have not gone away. The deterioration of our productivity and hence our competitiveness on the world market remains one of the gravest legacies of the Johnson era, a legacy that would lead within a few years to an insolvent America.

THE POSTWAR order, based on U.S. predominance in the West, was threatened not only by these ominous economic trends but also by new forces in the Third World let loose by the rebellion that broke out in Algeria on All Souls' Day, November 1, 1954. For the Western world, the consequences of the Algerian rebellion were to be significantly different from the results of the struggle for independence that had marked the British withdrawal in South Asia, the Dutch retreat from Indonesia and even the French defeat in Vietnam. For one thing, the guerrilla and terrorist success of the Algerian Arabs against their colonial rulers was not paralleled by any other Arab regime. An internal coup d'état marked the transition in 1952 from Farouk's to Nasser's Egypt. In Iraq, the postwar eradication of British control was not sudden and violent. Radical Arab regimes would often supplant conservative or moderate pro-Western regimes. But the Algerian rebellion was different.

Unlike the Vietminh in 1954, the Algerian rebels won their war against a large, well-equipped conscript French army. Among the Arabs, the success of the Algerian guerrillas in bringing a great European power to sue for peace gave to Algeria a prestige unequaled even by Nasser's Egypt. As far as the Arab world is concerned, as historian Alistair Horne predicted, "In terms of economic efficiency and accomplishment Algeria is the undisputed leader."[19] Thus, it was in Algeria in September of 1973 at the Conference of Nonaligned Nations that the provisions were first outlined for using the oil weapon in the form of an embargo against the West. That weapon was the indispensable arm of the Arabs in the Arab-Israeli War the following month.[20] Nor shall we soon have heard the end of the cry that the Algerians raised for equal shares between the rich and the poor nations.

The fall of the Fourth Republic as a result of the government's inability to put down the rebellion brought Charles de Gaulle to power. For the United States, de Gaulle came to mean the restoration of a strong France that openly contested American predominance in Western Europe. De Gaulle's France withdrew from NATO and vetoed British entry into the European Common Market, finally destroying Eisenhower's and Kennedy's "grand design" to bind the continent, Britain and the United States in an American-dominated Atlantic community.

Things would never be the same again between America and a Europe that challenged the United States both economically and now politically. The Atlantic Alliance endured, but after de Gaulle Washington could no longer take for granted Europe's willingness to follow an American strategy for the West. Today, Gaullism—no longer confined to France—survives as European nationalism largely directed against any return of American predominance, a movement that grows as the United States economy grows weaker and as the Soviet Union, at least in military terms, grows stronger. Nor is it likely to abate unless America is able to define and then defend her economic, military and political priorities.

THOUGH NONE of us in 1954 could have been aware that the settlement of the war in Southeast Asia was but a prelude to the second phase of the same conflict and that an inept uprising in North Africa was to become the most successful military campaign of the Arab world since the Arabs reached Grenada, as well as the harbinger of the Third World's cry for reparations, we clearly understood that the end of colonialism was at hand. But we could not know of other decisions made and not made that were to lead to greater global disorder from the point of view of American interests and to further decay of American dominance. As the year drew to a close French Prime Minister Pierre Mendès-France convened a cabinet-level interministerial meeting to discuss the military applications of atomic energy. A little over six years later, at the proving grounds of Reggane in the Sahara, the first French atomic bomb was exploded.

To be sure, the French program to develop atomic energy had begun immediately after the war, but until 1954 French policy was not aimed at making a bomb. What happened in 1954 is that the external situation had changed radically. The Soviets now possessed nuclear weapons and there were those in France who believed that America could no longer be counted on to defend European soil if her own cities were to become vulnerable to Soviet nuclear weapons. Moreover, the experience of the Indochina War, when Washington refused to employ nuclear weapons to break the siege of Dien Bien Phu, reinforced French doubts about America's willingness to defend the interests of her allies. Then, too, the fact of German rearmament, coupled with the possible eventual withdrawal of American troops from Europe, made a strong case for France to provide for her own security.[21] Indeed, as one historian aptly phrased it, "it would not be an overstatement to say that France developed her nuclear capability as much to save herself from her friends as to defend herself against her enemies."[22]

The French nuclear system was built without American aid and in the face of American disapproval. It may well have been an incentive for other nations to obtain nuclear weapons—India, Brazil, Israel, Argentina—and it has undoubtedly added to the problems of nuclear proliferation. France, like China, has refused to sign the nonproliferation treaty, and France, like China, guards her independence in planning her nuclear war-making strategy. Like the challenge from the Third World, whose use of the oil weapon has hampered the abilities of a superpower like the United States to impose its will by fiat, the challenge to superpower predominance by both France and China and the consequent spread of nuclear weapons gravely limits the ability of both superpowers to set up rules of the game that others must obey.

TO REGARD the world from a perspective of 1954, when America and Russia seemed both the inheritors and the guardians of the international order, was to imagine a future in which the definition and elaboration of America's vital interests would be centered on the U.S.-Soviet confrontation. This was true both with respect to America's attempts to counter Soviet ambitions and in her search for ways to deflect or divert them. Each recognized, albeit unwillingly, the other's sphere of influence in the Western Hemisphere and Eastern Europe. The protection of our allies in Western Europe and the Western Pacific was, by definition, the furthest extent of America's vital interests. Yet by the late

1950s the definition of our vital interests was becoming cloudy. We were beginning to extend our protection from the Mediterranean to Southeast Asia. Were these areas vital interests? It was never made clear to the American people that they were.

By the mid-1960s, the two superpowers were already competing in Asia and Africa and even in South America and the Caribbean for power and influence. As for Europe, the dramatic events of 1956—when the Soviet Union put down the Hungarian revolt with Soviet tanks and Washington lined up with Moscow to prevent Britain and France from seizing the Suez Canal after Nasser nationalized it—showed that the United States would not only respect Eastern Europe as a Soviet sphere of influence but would, if it chose to, thwart its allies. From that point on, it was clear that both America and Europe's perception of their vital interests would not necessarily coincide. Though Paris and London drew very different conclusions from the American response to the Suez fiasco—Britain eager to repair its "special relationship" with Washington; France determined to press on to construct her independent nuclear force—the basic European reaction to the events of 1956 was both to recognize the possibility of a sometime Russo-American partnership and to forestall such an eventuality by pushing forward toward some kind of grouping that would allow the Europeans freedom of action from the pressures of the superpowers. The Treaty of Rome establishing the Common Market, the embryo of the European Community, was signed the following year.

Meanwhile, the cold war continued—with occasional and

momentary pauses when it seemed as though the struggle between the two leviathans would give way to a spirit of peaceful competition and cooperation. Even the 1962 Cuban missile crisis—the most severe confrontation between the two superpowers since the Berlin blockade—was followed by the 1963 Test Ban treaty. Surely, at long last, a relaxation of tensions with the Soviet Union was beginning. And, indeed, both superpowers did sign a nuclear nonproliferation treaty in 1968. Nonetheless, America's growing involvement in Vietnam, as we supported Saigon and they Hanoi, and Moscow's brutal intervention in Czechoslovakia in 1968, postponed any significant progress on détente until it became evident that Nixon and Kissinger were prepared to liquidate the American military presence in Vietnam.

By 1980 we were far removed from the world of 1960, when the global containment of communism and the predominance of the dollar went virtually unchallenged. Then our interests seemed everywhere, and we hardly appeared to differentiate between our vital and our secondary interests. Today, we seem to have lost a sense of the enduring nature of our truly vital interests—those regions where U.S. security is directly affected—and how to safeguard them in the light of the unremitting rivalry between the United States and the Soviet Union. From the promise of détente in the beginning of the 1970s to the renewed cold war at the end, we have expended our energies in trying to manage a retreat from an overextension of our economic and military power—and all this in the face of a broken presidency and the challenge of Third World nationalism for a redistribution of world economic power. We now have to ask ourselves how we can conduct an intelligent foreign policy with our economic power seriously reduced, with no overriding domestic or foreign consensus, and no clear definition of our vital interests.

II

VITAL INTERESTS

Ever since the flood tide of American power in 1954—
and especially after the escalation of the Vietnam War
—America has been increasingly unable to define her vital
interests. And although America's overarching national interest is solvency at home and abroad, achieving it is a
particularly delicate and difficult task in a democracy which
does not perceive the depth of the crisis confronting it.

A democracy is built on shared values. The search for
consensus on national goals and the means to pursue them
necessarily comes from debating issues and arriving at an
overall agreement on what can be sensibly aimed at and
achieved. The model of democratic government for America has been the town meeting, where factions openly con-

tend, where all men and women may be heard and where a consensus finally emerges, but the larger model we have chosen for resolving our differences has been the republic. In our system of representative government, the forging of consensus by debate has been inherent since Madison, Jay and Hamilton argued the case in *The Federalist* for making a federal republic out of a confederation of states. Although the original colonies had already attained an inchoate political understanding by the end of the Revolution—"each individual citizen everywhere enjoying the same national rights, privileges, and protection"—the founders of our nation harbored no illusions, in an age rife with factionalism, that a consensus among the citizens would be easy to obtain. Hamilton warned us not to forget that "men are ambitious, vindictive and rapacious;" Madison argued that "the latent causes of faction are . . . sown in the nature of man, and we see them everywhere brought into different degrees of activity, according to the different circumstances of civil society"; and Washington himself believed that "few men are capable of making a continual sacrifice of all views of private interest or advantage to the common good."[1]

From the very beginning, then, we have understood both how difficult and how important it is to overcome factionalism if we are to manage our own political affairs. We have also seen factionalism triumph when disintegrative tendencies get beyond control by rational political means. Our history bears witness to the forces for disintegration as well as integration that have characterized the American Commonwealth. The tragic struggle for unity that culminated in the Civil War and the bitter battles between isolationists and interventionists before Pearl Harbor remain vivid in our historical memory.

After World War II, largely in response to the lessons of the interwar period when dissension among the democracies encouraged the totalitarian aggressors, America operated under a broad foreign policy consensus of containing Soviet and Chinese communist expansion. The Chief Executive—from Truman to Kennedy—implemented its foreign policy goals with little or no opposition from the Congress or special interest groups. Selling programs to Congress and the American people in this era was always made easier if they could be clothed in one garment. In 1947 the Truman administration's desire to provide aid to Greece and Turkey was sold to Congress as something larger than simply the containment of the Soviet Union in a particular area such as Europe and the Near East. In order to persuade a budget-conscious Republican Congress and an apathetic public of the dangers, President Truman drew a starkly dramatic picture—the very existence of the Greek nation threatened by Communist guerrillas—and this clash was only part of the global struggle "between alternative ways of life." "It must be the policy of the United States," said the President, in words that were to become known as the Truman Doctrine, "to support free peoples who are resisting attempted subjugation by armed minorities or by outside pressures."

It seems clear now that in seeking consensus for American aid against possible Soviet expansion in the Eastern Mediterranean, Truman used words that later opened the door to a broad American policy directed against communism whether it was expansionist or not. Aid and alliance to counter the threat from the Soviet Union in one region became, with the Korean War in 1950, a crusade against communism in virtually every corner of the globe. Moreover, largely as a result of that war, the struggle became defined as broadly based anticommunism rather than as the original confrontation with actual or perceived Soviet expansion.

It was, of course, the Vietnam War that broke the foreign and domestic consensus. This was the beginning of the end of the dream of limitless consumption and limitless expectations.[2] We lost our first modern war. We fell terribly in debt, and we debased our currency. Because Congress regretted endorsing the Chief Executive's escalation of a war without a declaration of war, the result was a withdrawal of blanket congressional support for the Executive to implement whatever foreign policy initiatives he chose to undertake. The 1973 War Powers Resolution, restricting the right of the President to commit U.S. forces abroad without explicit congressional approval, is the most telling example of how Congress has curtailed Executive initiative in foreign affairs. In the light of congressional restraints on U.S. actions abroad, such as the Senate vote to cut off funds for covert U.S. military aid to Angola in 1975, Kissinger went so far as to complain that "America seems bent on eroding its influence and destroying its achievements in world affairs." And during the Carter administration, Congress continued to assert itself in the making of foreign policy. In its debate over the Panama Canal treaties, its examination of arms sales to the Middle East, its reluctance to repeal the arms embargo to Turkey and to comply with the U.N. trade embargo against Rhodesia, to cite just a few examples, Congress showed that it would not automatically endorse presidential policies. The most dramatic refusal of that Congress to support a presidential initiative was, of course, its unwillingness to move swiftly to ratify the SALT II treaty on arms limitations concluded between Moscow and Washington, even before the Soviets invaded Afghanistan.

Much of this congressional intransigence can be explained as part of the legacy of both Vietnam and Watergate—clear examples of abuse of presidential power and, perhaps more important, explicit shows of dishonesty on the part of the Executive. The escalation of the Vietnam War was accompanied by misleading statements that the war was going well and that we were "winning"; Watergate speaks for itself. For these reasons alone, it is hard to imagine that the postwar consensus could have been resurrected during the 1970s.

By 1980, however, largely as a result of the new Soviet ability to extend its military reach into Africa and the Middle East, a new foreign policy consensus centering on anti-Sovietism—directed at the Russian nation rather than worldwide communist ideology—began to emerge in Congress. Moreover, if the Soviet Union were to appear so powerful in the Middle East that the oil-producing states would have to accommodate their policies to the wishes of the Soviet Union, the United States and its allies would find their access to vital resources controlled by their adversary, a development that would inevitably alter the world balance of power. In such circumstances, the Soviet Union could use oil as a potential weapon to try to break the American alliance with Europe and Japan, whose need for Persian Gulf oil renders them particularly vulnerable to this kind of pressure.

After the Soviet invasion of Afghanistan, which seemed to the Carter administration to confirm the Soviet Union's design on the oil-producing area, the overall foreign policy consensus that the administration itself sought also appeared to be based on collective anti-Sovietism. Whether the President needed a new energy bill calling for higher taxes on imported oil (which he did not get), or a higher defense budget to protect some of the oil we imported (which was easy to obtain), he invoked the threat of an expanding Soviet Union.

During the 1980 campaign, candidate Reagan, in effect, organized his own foreign policy pronouncements around the theme of anti-Sovietism, with even more sweeping judgments than Carter's. "Let us not delude ourselves," he said in an interview in *The Wall Street Journal.* "The Soviet Union underlies all the unrest that is going on . . . in the world."[3]

A foreign policy centered simply on anti-Sovietism makes no sense for the United States. We have many other foreign policy problems that profoundly affect our vital interests that either do not involve the Soviets directly or invite cooperation with them. An example of the first instance was our searing debate on turning over jurisdiction of the Panama Canal to the Panamanians, a debate which, stripped of its jingoist overtones, involved questions of America's strategic needs within her traditional sphere of influence; but no Soviet threat to the Canal was evident. Another example of a recent U.S. foreign policy problem that did not involve the Soviet Union was Washington's attempt to mediate the Greek-Turkish dispute and so to rescind the arms embargo to Turkey that Congress had imposed; although reconciliation between Athens and Ankara would certainly strengthen NATO, no immediate Soviet threat to either Greece or Turkey was apparent. Perhaps the most dramatic illustration of this was the 1980 Iraqi-Iranian war, which affected the interests of both superpowers but was instigated by neither.

In the second instance, anti-Sovietism is not at the center of such issues as the control of transnational forces that threaten international order—such issues as the environment, exploitation of the seabeds, nuclear proliferation and international terrorism. To deal effectively with these problems requires at the outset a recognition that there are overlapping alliances and shifting coalitions—and occasions where the United States and the Soviet Union may find themselves in the same boat or else both risk drowning in a sea of troubles.

Similarly, every Soviet move is not directed against us. Soviet willingness to use force to preserve its control over Eastern Europe—explicit in Hungary in 1956, in Czechoslovakia in 1968, and implicit during the negotiations between Polish leadership and the striking workers in 1980—is not directed against the United States, even as the guardian of Western Europe. But Soviet expansionism—even when it does not threaten us directly—is not something we should remain indifferent to. For example, Soviet support of Vietnam is primarily aimed at the containment of China—but there is always the danger that Vietnam, a Soviet ally, after expanding into Cambodia, might thrust into Thailand, whose government is aligned with ours. At that point, we would have to decide on the nature of our support for Thailand—do we provide military aid in dollars only or military advisers or actual troops on the ground? To answer these questions we would also have to determine the degree of our commitment, given our finite resources, to confront the Soviets in areas of marginal strategic interest.

Without embarking on a program of global military containment, we must nonetheless ask ourselves how to counter the Soviet Union when, as in the case of Afghanistan, it moves to consolidate its own sphere of influence and, in so doing, threatens the interests of the United States and the overall balance of power. The invasion of Afghanistan accomplished three things: the installation of a regime more subservient to the Soviet Union in order to defeat Afghan resistance to Soviet control; the further containment of China because of Afghanistan's proximity to Pakistan, a neighbor and ally of China; a thrust southward that enables the Soviets to threaten the oilfields of southern Iran and the Gulf as well as the sea lanes of the Indian Ocean.

In considering how to respond to the Soviet Union, the United States has to be aware of what it can and cannot do to demonstrate to the Soviets that their attempt to impose change through military force will have grave costs. For example, there are limits to the direct use of military force in the region: a concentration of U.S. naval power in the Indian Ocean could not force fanatical students in Teheran into releasing American hostages any more than it could stop the Soviet Union from sending troops into Afghanistan in order to impose Soviet-style law and order there. On the other hand, as Soviet specialist Robert Legvold has pointed out, Washington could—and should—provide military assistance to the Afghan rebels "on a scale sufficient to complicate sorely the light-infantry assaults of the Soviet forces."[4]

Beyond arming the Afghans for a protracted struggle, there are also diplomatic initiatives we can take that might be equally or more effective in thwarting Soviet ambitions in the area.[5] For example, we can work to encourage rapprochement between India and Pakistan that would surely blunt the Soviet policy of encircling China and inhibit any Soviet move into Pakistan to "clean out the rebels." We can thus show the Soviet Union that we understand its motivations and even explain to the Soviet leadership exactly what America is doing and why we are doing it.

To advance foreign policy goals involves not only devising military and diplomatic strategies to contend with the growing trend of a Soviet Union that seems bent on increasing its power and influence in the Third World, but also using our economic power to influence the behavior of other nations that may or may not be the objects of Soviet foreign policy. Yet our aid to less developed nations has decreased by 38 percent between 1961 and 1977. Futhermore, in both 1980 and 1981, Congress failed to approve even modest aid budgets, which, through the device of continuing resolutions, kept spending at the 1979 level. Similarly, at the end of the 1970s, our military assistance program grants and foreign military sales credits were 23 percent less, in constant dollars, than twenty years ago. Moreover, we concentrated our limited resources on two Middle Eastern countries—Israel and Egypt— which recieved 82 percent of total U.S. military assistance in 1979.[6] Even though, after the fall of Somoza, many in Congress feared that Nicaragua would become "another Cuba," i.e., a Soviet ally dependent on aid from Havana and Moscow, Congress itself delayed for almost a year approving and releasing a paltry $75 million in supplementary aid to the struggling new government.

While U.S. assistance programs cannot ensure political leverage over others, they can at least force the recipients to take account of America's interests and the incentives that such aid provides. Despite America's declining industrial power—which thirty years ago accounted for two-thirds of the world's production and now accounts for less than one-third—the United States still offers economic rewards far greater than any other power, whether in the form of aid, credits, private bank loans, trade or transfers of technology.[7] Compared to the United States, the Soviet Union is economically backward, a condition that makes it dependent on military force as the essential tool of its foreign policy. And yet the decline in relative U.S. economic strength, especially marked over the last decade by the slow growth of our productivity, might tempt us to concentrate our energies more and more heavily on military spending, mimicking to this extent our principal adversary. If we were to continue cutting back on aid and trade concessions as inducements to political cooperation while spending vast sums of money on new weaponry, we would simply deprive ourselves of valuable assets we should be using to advance our foreign policy interests.

What we are doing, in other words, is pursuing our old

game of guns and butter, insisting on a panoply of high-technology weapons as well as an ever-higher standard of living. It is like the policy we pursued in the days of cheap energy and an American trade surplus—only now the circumstances have radically changed, as energy costs rise and trade is in deficit. No wonder both our friends and adversaries are bewildered by our inability to make choices even when the consequences involve the security and well-being of the nation. They hear the President and the Congress talk of war in order to safeguard the oil routes in the Persian Gulf and the Caribbean; then they note that Congress is unwilling to impose even a modest gas tax to reduce the imports that everyone at home agrees constitute a clear and present danger to the national security.[8]

Our need in foreign policy as in domestic policy is to act in accordance with our means, distinguishing our vital from our general interests, and doing all we can, meanwhile, to improve our means without weakening our dollar. Unless we do so, we cannot advance or defend these interests. But we must first ask ourselves what these interests are.

OUR HISTORY has been one of abundance, not constraints. Our vital interests expanded globally as they had earlier expanded across a continent, and our economy did likewise. But, by our bicentennial, we were becoming insolvent, a danger Walter Lippmann warned us of in the middle of World War II when we were on our way to becoming a superpower. "For nations, as for families," he wrote, "the level may vary at which a solvent balance is struck. If its expenditures are safely within its assured means, a family is solvent when it is poor, or is well-to-do, or is rich. The same principle holds true of nations. The statesman of a strong country may balance its commitments at a high level or at a low. But whether he is conducting the affairs of Germany, which has had dynamic ambitions, or the affairs of Switzerland, which seeks to hold what it already has, or the United States, he must still bring his ends and means into balance. If he does not, he will follow a course that leads to disaster."

For a time, a great nation can live off its capital and borrow against its future, and the fact that it is no longer as productive as it once was can go unnoticed. This is no longer possible for the United States. In the past fifteen years, according to Henry Kaufman of the banking house of Salomon Brothers, our debts have tripled while the productive capacity to repay them has only doubled. By now, we owe $4.2 trillion in government, household and business debts, while the market value of America's productive facilities total only $1.2 trillion. In other words, as Jason Epstein pointed out in reviewing Kaufman's figures, "since 1964 we have borrowed slightly more than two dollars for every dollar's worth of productive capital we created. The other borrowed dollar we consumed or otherwise failed to use productively."[9] Our foreign policy, which is supposed to advance our national interest, does not exist autonomously; our ability to implement a meaningful foreign policy, with respect to Russia or even El Salvador, depends on the strength of our economy. Thus, even after we define our vital interests, we have to mobilize our resources to defend these interests. In short, we have to become solvent once again.

Today our vital interests encompass the defense of the

homeland, the integrity of those countries we see fit to defend, such as Europe, Japan and Israel, and access to our markets and source of supplies abroad, including, at least for a time, that part of the Third World called the Persian Gulf. Although it has become the conventional wisdom since the Vietnam War that the United States neither could nor should be the world's policeman, enforcing a *pax Americana*, we have failed to make clear distinctions between our vital and our secondary interests. Instead, we have continued to maintain existing commitments, even though our ability to honor them, if tested, has become increasingly suspect. This is the heart of our foreign policy problem.

AS WE REASSESS our place in a world we can no longer dominate, it is clear that we must always be able to defend our homeland, which requires, at the present time, a global defense to protect the sea and air lanes that give us access to our vital resources. In an age where technology has made it possible for nuclear armed missiles to travel thousands of miles, this has also meant maintaining strategic parity with any presumed adversary in the world. But if we were to rely on this strategy alone, and should deterrence fail, we would be left with only the threat of mutual suicide.

The defense of the homeland has to include the ability to counter threats to our own security without resorting to nuclear weapons, unless the Soviet Union uses them first. This strategy is particularly significant when it comes to threats posed by forces within the Western Hemisphere. The Kennedy administration believed that the Cuban missile crisis of 1962 represented just such a threat, not because the Soviet missiles being installed in Cuba were substantially more of a threat to us than Soviet-based long-range missiles but because Khrushchev's policy of intruding into an American sphere of influence broke the rules the two superpowers had presumably established when the United States accepted a Soviet sphere in Eastern Europe. Khrushchev was overthrown partly as a result of his adventuristic policy in the Caribbean, and the Soviet Union, determined to avoid another such humiliation when confronted by an American ultimatum backed up by an American naval blockade of Cuba, embarked on a worldwide naval build-up; but even as the Soviets expanded their military strength, they did not challenge us in our own hemisphere.

The geographical position of the United States is such that it should be able to protect itself in its own hemisphere without threatening the independence of others. We have long ago achieved what Hamilton said should be our aim, that is, to be ascendant in the system of American affairs. But this ascendancy need not include a presumption to interfere in the internal affairs of the other nations in the Western Hemisphere. Thus, we should be able to distinguish between those who pose actual military threats to our security and states whose governments, although they may be hostile to us, are not directly menacing. A decade ago, at a time when Kissinger did not regard Marxist Chile as a military threat, he described it sardonically as a dagger pointed at the heart of Antarctica; if he was right in speaking of it in those terms, then the Nixon administration was wrong in helping to overthrow the Allende government.

The Carter administration, for example, was wrong to

label as an "unacceptable" threat to our security a Soviet brigade in Cuba that had been there a number of years as a training unit. Even though this was a silly political ploy designed to counter right-wing charges of softness toward communism, it was a dangerous statement because it evoked a menace that did not really exist. By contrast, a Soviet fleet in the Caribbean that would threaten our sea lanes and access to raw materials, or a Cuban expeditionary force in Central America, would be true causes for alarm. In short, the United States, with preponderant economic and military power in its own hemisphere, needs to be especially prudent in exercising this power, particularly given the history of U.S. intervention in the affairs of its neighbors. For we have never been isolationist in the Western Hemisphere, and our economy dominates the region—for example, our largest trading partner is Canada, though by the mid-1980s Mexico might supplant her, and about 80 percent of our exports to developing countries go to Latin America.

Even taking into account the limitations on our economic and military power in the 1980s, our ability to protect our homeland has so far remained unimpaired against anything short of a Soviet nuclear attack. The greatest danger we face in the Western Hemisphere is likely to come from our tendency to misunderstand the nature of revolution in the region and to attribute the rise of left-wing, revolutionary regimes to the machinations of the Soviet Union and thus to frame policies for the hemisphere solely in terms of the cold war.

Beyond the northern half of the hemisphere, Western Europe and Japan remain vital to American interests—not only because, as democracies, we share moral and political values, but also because we have strong economic ties with each of them. Moreover, their economic and human resources in hostile hands would tip the balance of power against us. Our own well-being depends on the stability of these nations—hence our fear that an economic or social breakdown of Japan, Germany or France (which would then undermine the European Community) would directly affect us. And we have always believed that any Soviet expansion into these areas would be a direct threat to us.

Both in Europe and on the Korean peninsula the United States and the Soviet Union have worked out a series of constraints according to the limits of each side's power. Both sides have drawn lines, which neither can cross with impunity. When Eisenhower did not respond to the pleas of the Hungarians for aid in 1956, the United States accepted the de facto partition of Europe. Washington reaffirmed this policy in 1968 when the Soviets invaded Czechoslovakia; had Soviet troops intervened in Poland in 1980 to quell the striking workers, the United States would have made no overt military gestures to assist the Poles. Similarly, after the 1953 armistice in Korea the two sides have not seriously challenged the partition of the peninsula.

These lines should define America's vital interests in the Atlantic and the Pacific, extending as they do in Europe through Greece and Turkey, the southern extremities of the NATO command, and including, for many reasons, Israel. In the Far East, our defense remains what it should be—a Pacific defense, including islands from Japan to the Philippines, and with only a temporary presence on the mainland, notably in Korea. This assumes, of course, a stable Europe and Japan and a Soviet Union reluctant to violate the postwar order in those two areas. From an American perspective, maintaining these lines depends on the United States and its continuing alliance with Western Europe and Japan, not on the restraint or good will of the Soviet Union.

As for our relations with China, our interests cannot be served by establishing either an explicit or an implicit alliance with her. Nor is it in our national interest to push her into becoming a military power capable of inflicting serious damage on Russia, for this would also risk provoking Moscow into attacking China. Nor, finally, should we ignore the possibility that in the long run China might prefer to see America and Russia destroy each other, leaving the Middle Kingdom as the predominant world power, which it surely believes it should be. Thus, playing the "China card" to keep Russia preoccupied with her Eastern frontiers is a risky game for the United States. For example, the Carter administration, continuing the triangular diplomacy of the Kissinger years, went ahead toward full normalization of relations with Peking; but no sooner had this been done than China attacked Vietnam. Who, then, was playing the card against whom? Though Carter declared that he was following an even-handed policy toward China and the Soviet Union, from Moscow's perspective it seemed a policy of encouraging China in her attempt to humiliate Moscow's Vietnamese allies.

In Soviet eyes, there is already a balance of forces arrayed against her in northeast Asia, with China, Japan and America combining against the U.S.S.R. It is an impressive grouping, and one in which the United States is the preponderant military power. Thus, power in the Pacific is not in equilibrium, but rests on an American predominance that aims at the containment of the Soviet Union.

THE THIRD WORLD is not China. It is not an area like Europe and the Western Pacific where the superpowers can work out a program of mutual deterrence. It is not possible to draw lines there which an adversary would cross at its peril, because the Soviet Union—and often we ourselves—see the Third World as part of a general competition between the East and West. In a sense, these are vast territories up for grabs, because the opportunity to compete for control or influence is far greater than in a partitioned Europe.

As Seweryn Bialer has put it: "The Soviet concept of what is positive in the . . . Third World is opposite to that of the United States and the West. Not equilibrium, stability, and orderly change, but ferment, instability, and revolutionary upheavals. In fact, as long as conditions in the Third World and regional conflicts do not create the kind of tension that may lead to a direct confrontation between the superpowers and create a danger of a major East-West war, it is not much different from the former Chinese preference for 'heavenly disorder.' "

To the Soviets, whatever undermines the status quo in the noncommunist world is probably a trend in their favor. Thus, revolution and nationalist aspirations in the Third World almost always receive wholehearted Soviet support. Moreover, because of Soviet weakness in resources other than its military might, the U.S.S.R. tends to want to foment, escalate, or maintain conflicts rather than seek peaceful solutions to them, especially in the early stages where they can best be solved without resorting to military force. To gain what Bialer calls "their place in the sun," to achieve status and influence as well as the ideological and strategic superiority they crave, the Soviets will probably continue to intervene in the Third World even while seeking to mitigate tensions with the United States elsewhere. The danger in the 1980s is that the disorder will become less heavenly even for the Soviets, and that tensions between the superpowers may grow until direct confrontation between them becomes likely.

As a superpower, we have world-wide interests; so, too, do the Soviets. At times, certain areas will be more important to us than at other times: for example, Thailand or southern Africa on the brink of a race war, or, as now seems most probable after the Soviet invasion of Afghanistan, southwest Asia. Thus the Third World beyond the Western Hemisphere remains an area of serious American interest, but it becomes a vital interest only insofar as we or our allies remain gravely dependent on foreign natural resources. By this definition, the Persian Gulf region is a vital interest.

In becoming so dependent on imported oil we have dangerously extended the range of our vital interests to the point where the security of the Persian Gulf has become for us a matter of life or death. We have neither earned enough abroad to cover the ever-higher oil bills for imported oil nor significantly reduced oil imports. Had we been determined to do so, we could have combined higher earnings from the exports of our goods and services with reduced consumption of imported oil through both conservation and substitution, and so counterbalanced the oil price increases.[10]

We did not do so. We did just the opposite. Our oil imports nearly doubled between 1972 and 1978. Inflation rose along with consumption. As inflation rose, so did the cost of imported oil as the oil-producing countries hiked their prices. These price rises worked as a kind of foreign tax on the United States. They simultaneously reduced our capital for domestic investment, thus slowing growth, while raising the cost of energy even higher and thus contributing to higher inflation.[11] No explanations will ever suffice to make future generations understand the timidity of politicians who refused to say the game was over and that we had to conserve oil immediately, even if this meant imposing a stiff gasoline tax, or the draconian solution of gas rationing. Not to do so was folly even less explicable than the Vietnam War.

In both cases, we were profligate. Waging the Vietnam War to contain presumed communist expansion, we expended lives and treasure in an area that was hardly vital to our national interest. In refusing to curb imported oil, we not only put ourselves in economic jeopardy through inflation but we make ourselves dependent on oil supplies far from our shores, controlled by unstable governments adjacent to Soviet forces whose geographical proximity gives them a clear tactical advantage. Furthermore, our relations with our allies became gravely strained when we exhorted Germany and Japan in 1977 to stimulate their economies, even at the risk of inflation, although we had made little serious effort to reduce our oil dependency; in their eyes we are seen as the worst energy wastrel there is, while, even with their best efforts, continental Europe and Japan will remain vulnerable on the oil front for some time to come. They are truly dependent on Persian Gulf oil—Western Europe for about 60 percent of its oil imports and Japan for 70 percent. They are highly vulnerable to any oil cutoff. So are we—but we need not be if we take steps to reduce oil dependency in that part of the world.

The figures revealing our vulnerability to a cutoff of oil supply from the Persian Gulf present us with a fateful paradox: while we increase our reliance on potentially hostile oil producers, we are also in a position to remove this very dependence. At the end of the 1970s, for example, oil consumption was about 49 percent of total U.S. domestic energy consumption. Imported crude oil came to about 45 percent of the oil we consumed. Since Persian Gulf oil made up about 31 percent of these imports, this meant that this oil, highly vulnerable to a cutoff, constituted about 14 percent of total U.S. oil consumption,[12] or nearly seven percent of all the energy America consumes.[13] Moreover, since Persian Gulf oil is a dominant portion of the world oil export market, any cutoff from the area affects the price and availability of imported oil anywhere in the world. An American energy program to reduce our dependence on imported oil —and, in particular, Persian Gulf oil—would allow the United States a new freedom of action in countering Soviet or any other threats to the stability of the Persian Gulf region.

Even if the supply of oil from the Gulf were not vital to the United States, it would be vital to our allies in Europe and, especially, to Japan. Thus the Gulf remains a serious geostrategic U.S. interest, no matter what domestic energy policies we pursue. Nonetheless, by reducing our dependence on imported oil we ourselves would not be so vulnerable in the Gulf, and therefore would be free to act in whatever way might serve our own interests in protecting and promoting the oil flow to our allies. Moreover, by eliminating our own dependence on Gulf oil, we could then put it to our allies to take the lead in developing policies to ensure their own supply of oil from the region and for America to back them up by whatever political, economic and military measures we might deem necessary.

If both our allies and our adversaries—whoever they may be—realize that America is not dependent on Persian Gulf oil, not vulnerable to an oil cutoff, then they will appreciate that we have enormous freedom of maneuver to sustain our allies in their efforts to protect their continuing vital interests. For if it is clearly understood—and it should be—that the security of the European continent, Great Britain and the Western Pacific are vital to the security of the United States, then it must also be understood that we are willing and able to help our allies in the Gulf region if their interests there are truly threatened. This we can do most effectively if we ourselves are free from the constraints that dependence and vulnerability impose.

CLEARLY WE WILL not be able to protect our vital interests unless we restore a solvent economy. But nothing seems more remote than our will to do just that. We have believed we could do everything. We are like proud parents who want their children to think that providing for them in a grand way is something easily and gracefully done, something that involves no sacrifice and no sweat. So we made no cutbacks in our commitments to ourselves or to our allies. We made no concessions in our claims to be able to protect and provide for everyone. When we became increasingly less competitive in the 1970s—with declining productivity and growing inflation—we did nothing to meet that problem as we continued to finance the growth of factories outside America where labor was cheap, machinery was new, and productivity was rising. In this way, American investment abroad not only provided modern technology for other countries but also allowed us, for example, to make our television sets abroad with cheap labor and then sell them to ourselves for less than they would have cost if they were made at home. At the same time, we did not create conditions in the United States to encourage capital formation—from whatever source—that would have promoted investment in new industries and kept America in a high competitive position.

By the end of the decade, many of our manufactured goods had become less desirable even though many of them had become cheaper to buy. Because we had not invested enough in modernizing our plants, the quality of some of our durable manufactured goods deteriorated and they were no longer preferred as they had once been, either abroad or even at home. According to polls, in 1980 nearly 50 percent of Detroit's engineers believed that the Japanese produced the best cars in the world.[14]

Our response to losing markets for our goods has been to protect ailing domestic industries, such as the once-proud steel and auto industries, by restricting imports through tariffs and quotas and relying on markets at home, or within our own sphere of influence, that are receptive to our goods. To seek wholly national solutions such as these might seem in the short term a welcome respite from competition from other advanced industrial or newly industrializing societies threatening our domestic industries with cutbacks or even extinction and thereby raising the level of unemployment. But in the long term these policies will produce a world of competing national states or groupings, each of which will impose its own trade barriers; this in turn will lead to a further deterioration of our domestic industries, freed from the need to confront foreign competition.

In the steel and auto industries, it is not a question of competing with cheap foreign labor, for by 1978 the U.S. average earnings were only six percent higher than in Germany and Japan.[15] It is a matter of efficiency, of worker productivity, of antiquated plants, of poor management committed to quick profits rather than long-term investment, and a government that held gasoline costs at an artificially low level, encouraging auto-makers to build fuel-inefficient cars. Of the seven major economies in the noncommunist world since the mid-1960s—Japan, Germany, France, Italy, Canada, the United Kingdom and the United States—the American economy has had the lowest annual growth in real gross national product per employed worker, a telling index of American productivity. For example, Japan heads the list with 3.4 percent growth per worker from 1973 to 1979, whereas the United States is at the bottom, with only 0.1 percent, the weakest of the lot in its ability to deliver gains in productivity.[16] With declining productivity come higher unit labor costs since business cannot offset higher payroll costs with increased production per worker. The result is more inflation in retail prices of manufactured goods.

Today the average U.S. plant is twenty years old, compared to the average in Germany of twelve years and in Japan, ten years. One way we can improve our rusting industrial plant and provide employment for workers who otherwise may have to be laid off is to encourage foreign investment in specific sectors—such as the automotive assembly factories that Volkswagen has built in Pennsylvania and Honda is planning in Ohio.[17] But encouraging foreigners to restore American productivity is inadequate if we are to improve our competitiveness in the world market. We must be able to compete with products from other industrialized societies; otherwise we will find that our own industrial base will stagnate further.

We still depend on high-technology products for many of our exports—about 40 percent of our exported manufactured goods at the end of the 1970s.[18] Clearly, the United States must continue to innovate in order to remain in world markets. Yet though the proportion of U.S. resources devoted to research and development is higher than anywhere else, it is becoming a declining fraction of our gross national product, while it has been rising in Germany, Japan and France, our main competitors. These countries, moreover, have devoted far smaller proportions of research and development to defense than the United States and have instead concentrated on research that applies to civilian production

—a pattern that also helps to explain the relative decline in productivity and competitiveness in the United States.[19]

In these circumstances, a rational strategy for encouraging competition among advanced industrial societies would be to look ahead to determine what industries are likely to grow stronger and encourage them. This is what Japan tries to do, whereas the United States moves to protect its weaker ones. When Japan's annual economic survey indicates where the imports of certain goods are rising, the ministry of trade and industry concludes that such goods made in Japan represent a dying industry. For example, over the past few years the Japanese have come to believe that their transistor radios are a dying industry. When an industry like this appears on the endangered list, the bankers refuse to extend too much credit to manufacturers of transistors, since they may not get their money back. Particularly if the economy is growing too fast—with resulting inflation—and banks see the need to cut lending, they will stop lending first to endangered companies like the ones that make transistor radios.

The United States, like Italy and Great Britain, tends to do the opposite, protecting endangered industries in order to prevent unemployment. But Japan's policy cannot simply be transplanted to America. The United States has a far stronger trade union movement than Japan does, and a vaster, far less homogenous population, including large numbers of unskilled workers, and huge industrial regions that cannot be abandoned except at great financial and social costs.[20] It also has a welfare system that encourages the unemployed worker to remain unemployed.

Consider an unemployed welfare client in the South

Bronx wearing a shirt made in Central America or India because the shirt factory in his neighborhood had to close down in the face of this kind of foreign competition, and no comparable work was available. Like the country at large, he is consuming without producing, using imports he can't pay for out of his own productivity. It is simplistic to say that the marketplace will provide new jobs for him, for his skills may not be up to working in a higher technology industry than the shirt factory. Under these circumstances would it not be better to employ the worker—and make sure his after-tax wage is higher than his welfare or unemployment payments—even if this means subsidizing a local shirt factory so that it can compete with goods produced by cheap labor abroad?

In the near term, this may be the only rational choice. But we have agreements with other nations that make this difficult, and, too often, the temporary becomes permanent. Moreover, we have traditionally had a mobile labor force, and policy should be directed at increasing its movement both in location and in skills. Nonetheless, for workers faced with unemployment because of competition from newly industrializing countries of the Third World, as well as from rich industrial societies, some form of protectionism may be needed until new work opportunities can be found and workers trained for this purpose. At the same time, to avoid stagnation the government should provide incentives for modernizing our industrial plant so that new industries can spring up.

In both cases, in America today we are prey to drift and generally find ourselves faced with choices involving one or another form of subsidy. We end up subsidizing workers in a factory whose goods are being undersold by competition from poor countries, or subsidizing workers through unemployment or welfare payments, or—in the worst case—extending credits to industries that seek shelter from healthy competition from nations whose standards of living approach our own.

Even if industry and labor show enough common sense to agree on a policy that would encourage new industries and remodel the old, no such policy can be successful in improving our performance abroad unless we first bring inflation under control. With inflation, our trade balance grows worse as we consume higher-priced imports—and, in particular, imported oil. With increasing inflation, any incentive to save disappears, thus reducing the nation's effective source of funds—as distinct from the supply of printed money—available for industrial investment, which, in turn, restricts the improvements in productivity we claim to be seeking.

Instead of seeking solutions at home, we have preferred to use the fact that with 75 percent of all world business conducted in dollars we can still inflict our trade and budget deficits on the rest of the world. For a time, then, both nations and individuals may still have to accept our dollars, but they are beginning to turn them in for German marks —or for that traditional hedge against disaster, gold—because they have lost confidence in America's ability to manage her economy. The grave doubts that they feel about the American economic performance make foreigners—both adversaries and friends—equally uncertain of America's ability to achieve her political goals. And so, if we are to pursue an effective foreign policy, we must not only define our goals but define them in terms of our means.

HERE THE dangers to the United States of a huge increase in arms should be clear. To strengthen our economy our first goal must be to reduce our spending on overseas oil, in particular oil from the unstable Middle East. Until we have an effective energy policy, we cannot rebuild our industrial base and thus regain our ability to conduct a flexible foreign policy. Yet while we do little or nothing about oil we are determined to increase defense spending during a period of increased and probably prolonged tension with the Soviet Union, with defense costs likely to rise beyond expectations over the next few years, as they did during the Vietnam War.

For fiscal year 1982, beginning in October 1981, the outgoing Carter administration requested defense appropriations totaling nearly $200 billion, and the Reagan administration was committed to ask for an increase of about 12 percent over this amount. Over the next five years, through fiscal 1986, Carter's defense blueprint called for cumulative spending up to $1.27 trillion. Moreover, while Carter proposed increasing defense spending by about five percent a year in real dollars, some Senate Republicans advocated a seven percent increase. Assuming a ten percent rise in inflation—two percent less than the forcast for 1981—the costs for such a Republican program could rise to nearly $330 billion per year by the end of Reagan's first term.[21] In addition, Carter's budget request provided no allowance for increased costs of fuel—costs that will be asked for later. Nor does defense spending, since it is based on fulfilling a contract rather than competing for profits, generally improve productivity. What this probably means is a higher federal deficit, higher unemployment in non-defense industries, and a greater inflation rate than ever, because military spending does not increase the supply of U.S.-produced goods available to the consumer.

Thus we shall continue to rely on imports to maintain our standard of living, and if we do not expand our exports, that reliance will increase any balance-of-payments deficits. The greater the resulting deficits the more likely foreigners are to move their reserves out of dollars. This, in turn, can force the Federal Reserve Bank to raise interest rates to attract foreign capital in the hope of strengthening the dollar, as it did in 1980. High interest rates, however, hurt nondefense investment. Moreover, such high rates anger our allies, who then have to raise their own interest rates to prevent their currencies from being drained away. Meanwhile, politicians, reacting to pressures from all sectors of the electorate, demand a return of low interest rates; as soon as this happens, the dollar weakens again on the foreign exchanges and adds to inflation as we import goods that cost more and more with dollars worth less and less. The cycle begins again.[22]

In effect, we have a return to the Vietnam economic syndrome. Like the Johnson administration, the American governments of the 1980s may choose to increase spending for military hardware without seriously raising taxes—or, equally, if not more important, dramatically cutting energy consumption. The result of such a policy will be more inflation, and a far more troubled economic environment than we experienced in the 1960s.

Even in the short term, it is questionable whether we can

readily support a newly developing cold war. Only a drastic shift from civilian to military priorities can accomplish this. But without a declaration of national emergency, how will the United States mobilize the industrial capacity to produce the hardware the defense budget calls for? In defense, as in other industries, the underlying industrial base has continued to deteriorate since the Vietnam War.[23] The situation in defense inventories is so serious that in the weeks immediately following the Soviet invasion of Afghanistan the administration could not have kept its promises to furnish Pakistan with $400 million in hardware without stripping the U.S. armed forces of tanks, artillery, helicopters and other matériel.[24]

Beyond the inadequacies of our industrial base lies a serious debate among defense specialists over what we need for the defense of our vital interests and a fundamental question of how we can afford to pay for it. In short, what are we willing to give up to get what? A study by the Heritage Foundation, a conservative and influential think tank, calls for a major drive for added nuclear strength, including building the MX mobile missile, in order to prevent U.S. land-based missiles from becoming vulnerable to a Soviet first strike, which would theoretically become possible in the mid- to late 1980s. In addition, President Reagan has talked of reviving the program for the advance B-1 bomber, going ahead with the construction and deployment of the cruise missile, and the need for a three-ocean navy so that we can have a substantial naval capibility in the Indian Ocean as well as in the Pacific and Atlantic. Added to that is the immediate need to repair and refurbish our conventional forces. The costs of such a program are likely to far exceed even the seven percent increase already proposed—and all this at a time when the new administration promises to reduce inflation and aim for a balanced budget.

Even to begin to achieve these defense goals would require spending a far greater percentage of America's gross national product on defense than we now do—which runs to just under six percent of GNP. Professor Robert W. Tucker, in an article entitled "America in Decline," notes that in wartime 1944, defense spending was 45 percent of our gross national product, and in 1954, 14 percent. He believes we can certainly spend between eight and ten percent of our GNP on defense, a level "well below the portion spent during the years of the early 1950s" when "the dangers we face today are markedly greater than those we faced in the earlier period."[25] But the dangers of inflationary pressures under such a defense posture are also very great, as Tucker himself admits; and, as we have seen, the productive forces of this country have suffered a serious decline relative to those of other countries since the 1950s.

In order to reduce the prospect of inflation, which would disastrously weaken America's economy and hence her ability to provide a large part of Western security needs, a more modest program is clearly needed. But in the face of the recent buildup of Soviet forces, what kind of defense program would avoid sacrificing our economy to an inflationary military buildup while at the same time providing the most efficient defense possible for an America whose resources are not limitless? James Fallows and others have cogently argued that in order to improve our "real defense," and in view of our finite resources, each path we choose should eliminate several others. He and other analysts have sharply challenged the need for many of the new weapons systems that the Reagan administration may well want to build. Their most striking and strongly argued suggestion is for abandoning of ceasing to improve land-based intercontinental missile systems, such as the Minuteman, precisely because of their vulnerability. It would mean not building the mobile—and therefore less vulnerable—MX missile, a saving of between $30 and $100 billion, according to various estimates. This would still leave us with two other legs of our "nuclear triad"—long-range bombers carrying nuclear weapons, clearly less vulnerable than fixed, land-based missiles; and nuclear-missile submarines, "the least vulnerable weapons system," because of its extreme mobility and its almost perfect concealment under the oceans.

To save vast sums of money as well as increase our strength relative to the Soviets, we could build, as some defense specialists have argued, cheap mini-submarines that carry only a few missiles each, deploying them from 100 to 300 miles from our coastline, where we would have excellent communications and maximum protection from Soviet antisubmarine forces. This fleet would supplement our longer range, ocean-going submarines,[26] save money and provide a nearly invulnerable strategic weapons system.[27] It would be dangerous not to explore such programs fully and openly, before undertaking huge investments in land-based strategic weapons.

It would also be dangerous to accept current claims that the United States and its allies are falling behind the Soviet

Union in their military power. Despite the Soviets' increasing new military capabilities and the evident ability of the Russians to project military power far from their shores, we are not yet in a position of overall military inferiority to the Soviet Union. In nuclear forces in 1980, the United States outgunned the Soviet Union, by approximately 10,000 nuclear warheads to Moscow's 6,000. The Soviets may have more combat aircraft but our aircraft are of better quality. The Soviet Union's navy is growing but it does not possess the fire power we have.[28]

According to the 1979 *Strategic Survey* of the London-based International Institute of Strategic Studies, the United States and its NATO allies spend more money for defense than do the U.S.S.R. and its East European satellites—by $180 billion to $160 billion. If we add the Japanese contribution, the Western advantage is even greater. Moreover, about one quarter of the Soviet defense effort is directed at China. As for America's share in NATO's expenses, in 1979 the United States was spending about five percent of its gross national product on defense while its NATO allies were spending an average of 3.5 percent. With Western European industrial capacity almost equal to America's, this arrangement could be revised. If, therefore, the other NATO nations, as well as Japan, spent the same percentage of GNP on defense, the overall alliance defense expenditures would increase by 36 percent or $67.6 billion.[29]

Our near-term needs lie far less in the strategic realm than in the conventional. The United States should not be in its present situation, where so much is earmarked for the

NATO area that we must subtract from these forces to meet contingencies elsewhere. To protect our vital interests, particularly in the Persian Gulf, we need a convincing number of well-equipped mobile troops who could intercede if the main oil-producing countries were about to fall under control hostile to the United States and to its allies. The very existence of such forces would provide the most effective assurance that they would not have to be used. But this does *not* mean the United States should return to a policy of global intervention in which it would be committed to fight land wars throughout, for example, the southern parts of Asia, Africa, and Latin America. Our interests in these regions may justify diplomatic assistance and economic aid to governments that can make good use of it but not the sort of military adventure that so weakened the United States in the past.

Defense experts Barry Posen and Stephen Van Evera suggest four major reforms to improve the combat-readiness of our undermanned, undertrained and underpaid troops that the Chief of Staff has called "a hollow army."[30] They consist of better maintenance of older weapons systems; more equipment prepositioned in Europe; shifting more army manpower from support to combat roles; and producing more simply designed equipment. These are not proposals for huge weapons systems but for changes toward a more efficient fighting force. Again it would be irresponsible to embark on an arms buildup without fully exploring such concrete reforms.

With respect to conventional arms, our claim that we outdistance the Soviets in quality of weaponry, if not in quantity, is certainly hollow. For example, the current U.S.

tank, the M60, appeared in 1959. Though the Soviets enjoy a five-to-one superiority in tanks, since 1965 they have also introduced four new models, each one a significant improvement over the last. By the time the United States produces its radically new XM-1 tank in 1982 at the earliest, the Soviets will probably be deploying a new and improved version of their current model. In most instances, it would be far better for the United States to improve progressively its conventional weapons rather than spend years to devise brand-new, high-technology replacements. Less complex and more practical weapons in greater numbers are what we need if we are to show convincingly that we have the forces to prevent land warfare from breaking out in either Europe of the Persian Gulf. In essence, we are faced with the prospect of fighting a conventional war we can hardly afford or a nuclear war we cannot permit.[31]

Under current conditions, one of the swiftest—though not necessarily the cheapest—ways to improve the quality of our conventional forces would be to have a low-paid conscript army in the service of the national interest, with highly paid noncommissioned and commissioned officers. Under an all-volunteer army system, we simply do not possess the army reserves needed to reinforce or replace troops on the battlefield in any prolonged engagement. Paradoxically, while we have tried to make up for our lack of numbers by relying on a mechanized, "capital-intensive" army, this has meant depending on highly trained soldiers and the immediate use of reserves from the homeland. While it is difficult to make hard judgments on the quality of our manpower, it is clear that Army Reserve units have declined in strength, since they were formerly sustained by men enlisting as an alternative to active service and by those individuals serving out a four-year reserve obligation after two years on active duty. The situation is even worse in the Individual Ready Reserve where individuals are designated as replacements until full-scale mobilization goes into effect. William Hauser, in analyzing the nature of the hollow army, points out that the all-volunteer army has failed to provide "a genuinely capable reserve component." Instead, we have reduced soldiers on active duty to whatever level can be recruited voluntarily by relying on reserves to back them up, only to find the entire approach jeopardized because sufficient reserves are unavailable. "Because of increased reliance on reserves," Hauser concludes, "the nation's strategic commitments cannot be met in wartime. This is the central strategic issue which erodes strategic policy."[32]

In considering levels of defense spending, we are confronted with the image we have of ourselves as the other superpower, the guardian of the West. Clearly, we are still the leading opponent of the Soviet Union, whose pretensions to world leadership inevitably conflict with our own. Yet we appear irresolute, unwilling to pay the price for the defense of our vital interests. Nothing more starkly revealed the Carter administration's incompetence to defend these vital interests than the statements surrounding the enunciation of the Carter doctrine after Afghanistan. At first, the President declared the Persian Gulf region (not carefully defined) as vital to American interests, saying that the United States would repel an assault on the area by any means necessary—including military force. But less than a week later he admitted that neither "at this time nor in the future [do] we expect to have enough military strength and enough military presence to defend the region unilaterally." In these two statements Carter inadvertently summed up the devastating gap between our commitments and our capabilities that I have been describing in this book.

In a visit to the Soviet Union in 1980, I talked to a number of Soviet officials and academicians whose awareness of America's economic difficulties led them to conclude that we would be unwilling to keep up a high level of defense spending in the decade ahead. They see us repeating once again our experience with Vietnam and the oil crisis—an unwillingness to make the sacrifices necessary to strengthen the economy. In this respect they believe that we will demand both guns and butter and, if necessary, resort to the printing press to provide them.

The Soviets, too, see us lagging behind in productivity and believe it will become more and more difficult for us to compete in the world market. To do so, after all, requires considerable investment in new industries to develop competitive products for export, and they believe this is not likely to happen if we keep up a high level of military spending in order to rival their own military buildup. High military spending may also require cuts in social services that, they feel sure, will further strain the social fabric of the United States. Of course, one way to maintain the public sector is to borrow more, but this—absent the willingness of Americans to consume less but produce more—would intensify inflation and weaken the American system still more.

Under this analysis, the strain on the U.S. economy will

become so great that there will be calls to decrease military spending and for new initiatives on our part to reopen the road to détente. The Soviets simply do not believe that Americans possess the political will to repair their economy, so that in their view American defense spending will probably be determined less on an assessment of Soviet power than on how much the politicians feel can safely be taken away from the American consumer without losing his vote.

What the Soviets fail to understand is that U.S. military spending may increase precisely because the United States perceives a threat from the Soviet Union and will rearm even if this results in significant cuts in the social sector, less investment for new industries or even higher inflation. To assume that a troubled economy will lead the government to disarm is dangerous wishful thinking, with little historical basis. Indeed, Germany did just the opposite in the 1930s. But the Soviet analysis does reinforce the dire need for the United States to demonstrate the political will to reform and repair its economy, not by going further into debt by unrestricted consumption but by raising the productive level of its industry. If we do so, choices on how to maintain an effective defense establishment can be made without unduly straining the economy, and the road back to détente will be a path chosen rather than one forced upon us by our inability to arrive at a reasonable consensus on domestic and foreign policy.

There is a hard reckoning for an insolvent foreign policy. Commitments, in the final analysis, can only be validated by war. Insolvency, as Lippmann points out, means that "preventable wars are not prevented, that unavoidable wars are fought without being adequately prepared for them, and that settlements are made which are the prelude to a new cycle of unprevented wars, unprepared wars, and workable settlements."[33]

III

THE PRICE OF
SURVIVAL

I T IS A frightening truth that despite our continuing inability to manage our domestic economy and our consequent problems in providing a broad spectrum of defense
capabilities, American military power is the principal force
available to contain Russia in the East as well as in the West.
In protecting our vital interests under these conditions,
nothing would be more dangerous for us than to find ourselves with our alliances in splinters. An isolated America,
bristling with high-technology weapons, could only too easily find herself in a nuclear end game with the Soviet Union.

At this point, we are far from that deadly scenario. But
if we were to embark on a new policy of trying militarily to
contain the Soviet Union worldwide, the strains in our al-

liances would get far worse, not only because European and American strategies on how to deal with the Soviet Union are often vastly different but also because the costs of such a policy would be so high that our ability to provide for the bulk of our allies' security would be suspect. As a basis for policy, therefore, anti-Sovietism will divide us from our allies, and global military containment will exhaust us as we seek military superiority over the Soviet Union—the only way such a policy can be implemented.[1] To maintain military parity with the Soviets will be costly enough; a quest for military superiority would mean such a vast diversion of our resources into military spending that our standard of living would doubtless fall as the nondefense sector of our economy shrank.

Despite the dangers to the national interest that such a policy would entail, the Reagan administration may be sorely tempted to pursue this line of reasoning. Far from defining the defense of our vital interests outside the Western Hemisphere as the maintenance of our alliances with Western Europe and Japan—to say nothing of trying to ensure a continuing supply of oil from the Persian Gulf— President Reagan's foreign policy and defense task force concluded that "no area of the world is beyond the scope of American interests" and that the United States would need to have "sufficient military standing to cope with any level of violence" around the globe.[2] By implication, this language defines a world in which America could attempt to become once again its policeman. In such a world the distinction between our vital and our secondary interests will blur, and in the effort to reimpose a *pax Americana* we will risk losing our ability to defend ourselves beyond the Western Hemisphere.

As it is, there are—to a degree rarely seen in the past—serious divisions within the Atlantic Alliance over both the nature of the threat from the Soviet Union and how to deal with it. If this leads to a fragmenting of the alliance—the Soviet dream and the American nightmare—it is most likely to come out of this fundamental quarrel. To such Europeans as Giscard d'Estaing and Helmut Schmidt, the Soviet military threat is real and apparent—in Europe. To most Americans, the Soviet threat is far broader—directed at American interests in Europe and in the Far East, potentially menacing to the oil reserves of the Persian Gulf region, and ready to take advantage of any opportunity for political or ideological expansion in the Third World. To many Europeans, the Soviet Union appears as a bear entangled in a net of problems and all the more dangerous for that reason—bewildered about how to deal with a faltering economy, concerned over its diminishing energy reserves, anxious over the instability of its restive East European satellites, unable to extricate itself from a brutal war in Afghanistan, fearful of a hostile and now modernizing China and confronted by its still powerful rival, the United States, now preparing for a new round of military spending.[3] To most Americans, the Soviet Union thrusts outward, taking advantage of turmoil in southern Africa and Southeast Asia, starting to expand southward through Afghanistan to enlarge its empire, prepared to reassert its will by military force over any serious sign of rebellion in Eastern Europe and embarked on an arms build-up that aims at military superiority over the United States.

In the past, a Soviet threat tended to unify the alliance —for example, the 1962 Cuban missile crisis and hostile Soviet behavior in Berlin. Today, even when the Europeans denounce the Soviet invasion of Afghanistan, the alliance remains divided. Although Chancellor Schmidt has said that the danger of blundering into a war was greater in 1980 than at any time since 1914, he also believes the way to combat that danger is to emphasize arms control, and to expand trade and financial credits to the East bloc, so that inevitable tensions and confrontation with the Soviets do not escalate into war—in short, to pursue détente!

Many Europeans saw in the Soviet restraint toward events in Poland during 1980 evidence that their policy of détente had inhibited Soviet intervention; and even were the Soviets eventually to intervene in Poland, some European governments would not necessarily see this as the final breakdown of détente, though public opinion might insist that it was and prevail. The Soviets would surely justify any such action on narrow grounds and hope that their behavior would merely interrupt the détente process. There is, of course, no way of knowing if this policy would succeed; it might if it were confined to Poland. The final blow would undoubtedly be any Soviet intervention in East Germany—the *coup de grace* to Bonn's policy of resolving the issue of reunification by ever closer trade and freedom of movement between the two Germanys. Although armed Soviet intervention in Poland would temporarily unify the alliance, the endemic problems would remain—but with this difference. Soviet intervention would surely solidify the U.S. anti-Soviet consensus while the likely European attempt to revive détente after a decent interval would further strain the alliance, though perhaps not yet to the absolute breaking point. The United States has a very different strategy from West Germany and France toward dealing with the Soviet threat. Détente is no longer seen as a way of blunting Soviet adventurism; indeed, Soviet behavior in the 1970s seemed to confirm the failure of détente. The American response has thus been to stop trying to pursue or expand détente. Instead, the Carter administration curtailed most of our trade with the Soviets, reduced contacts, postponed sending a SALT II treaty to the Senate for ratification, and, most significant of all, increased arms spending. During his campaign, President Reagan urged an even greater arms buildup and insisted on a renegotiation of the SALT treaty. Even if the Reagan administration negotiates new arms control agreements, it is not likely to try to modify Soviet behavior by initiating a new policy of détente. The remilitarization of America has begun.

Unable therefore to find common ground in confronting the Soviet Union, the United States and Europe enter the 1980s with profound cleavages between them. Nor is it likely that we can bridge the gap between ourselves and our principal allies easily. The economic prowess of Europe and the relative weakness of the American economy only point up the contrast in the overall balance between Europe and America in economic relations and the grave imbalance in military matters.

After Afghanistan, the political differences between the United States and its allies were such that we are now forced to recognize the high degree of fragmentation in the Western world—a world that had already shown its disarray through conflicting policies toward the Middle East in a vain attempt to assure stable pricing and a steady supply of oil, and arguments over economic policies to control inflation and stimulate growth.

The U.S. response to Afghanistan was to cancel participation in the Moscow Olympics, as well as grain sales and industrial contracts worth an immediate $3 billion. Europe refused to take a common stand toward participation in the Olympics and, far from joining in an embargo on trade and technology, rushed to expand its already growing trade with the Soviets. Instead of cutting back ties with the U.S.S.R. in the six months following the Soviet invasion of Afghanistan, West Germany expanded its exports to Russia by 30 percent.[4] Likewise, in the first nine months of 1980, French-Soviet trade increased almost 60 percent. Of the only two major contracts won by the United States from the Soviet Union over the past five years—a $350 million electric steel plant for Armco (a joint venture with Nippon Steel of Japan) and a $100 million aluminum plant for Alcoa— both were canceled by the U.S. government after Afghanistan. This was not the end of the story, and what happened subsequently reveals the competitive nature of U.S.-European relations and the sharply differing ways of dealing with the Soviet Union.

Shortly after the Soviet invasion of Afghanistan, President Carter, in announcing a ban on strategic exports to the U.S.S.R., received assurances from the French and our other allies that they would not move in to fill any breaches created by suspension or cancellation of projects undertaken by American firms. Nonetheless, the French firm of Creusôt-Loire, whose bid had been lost to Armco, accepted the Soviet contract once the U.S.-Japanese firms were canceled out. In short order, the U.S. Treasury banned the import of certain products made by the French steel company, in a clear though unstated retaliation for France's unwillingness to follow U.S. policy denying any significant transfer of Western technology to the Soviet Union.[5]

The stakes are high in European-Soviet trade. By the end of the decade, the European Community exported about three times more to the Soviet Union than we did; the Europeans also took in about the same dollar volume of imports from the Soviet Union while ours were negligible. Moreover, by 1980 both France and West Germany were importing over four percent of their oil from the U.S.S.R. By the mid-1980s, West Germany will be importing about 30 percent of its natural-gas needs from the Soviet Union, and Western Europe as a whole 25 percent. In the European Community, imports from the Soviet bloc in coal, oil and natural gas came to between five and six percent of the Community's total primary energy consumption, roughly equivalent to U.S. energy consumption from Persian Gulf oil.[6] The Soviet Union had also become the largest supplier of enriched uranium to France—whose commitment to nuclear power as a source of energy is greater than any other nation's. For Western Europe, imports from the Soviet Union are critical to European economic well-being; for the Soviet Union, the hard currency earned in the West buys it the high technology and grain needed to keep its economy from falling into even graver straits than it already has.

The other area where the United States and Europe collide is in policy toward the Middle East. With Western Europe dependent on Persian Gulf oil for over 60 percent of its imports, the allies are concerned over ensuring the supply of oil from the region and being able to sell enough industrial goods to the suppliers to be able to pay for it. In practical terms, this has meant that the Europeans have been willing to sell the oil sheiks anything from nuclear reactors to supersonic jets. France—the world's third largest arms exporter after the United States and the Soviet Union—has been especially zealous in pushing the arms trade in this area; Saudi Arabia and Iraq, the two biggest suppliers of oil to France, are also France's best arms customers.[7]

Though France and other European countries merely compete with the United States in selling arms to the Arabs, political differences with Washington arise when the Europeans urge concessions by the Israelis to the Palestine Liberation Organization. While this policy may someday help to lay the groundwork for an overall peace settlement and thus help ensure Israeli security—a commitment both the United States and its allies share—it is futile to expect such a policy to work when it is linked to ensuring a supply of oil from the Middle East. David Watt, Director of the Royal Institute of International Affairs, claims that "the settlement of the Palestinian conflict would do more to secure Western oil supplies than any other single development that could be devised."[8]

It is hard to see how this is in any way self-evident. Neither the fall of the Shah, nor the Iraqi-Iranian War—both of which seriously interrupted oil supplies as well as pushing up prices—had anything to do with the Palestinian

issue. Even the 1973 Arab oil embargo, organized by the
Arabs primarily to show solidarity with the Egyptians and
Syrians who were doing the actual fighting during the Arab-
Israeli War, did not prevent oil from flowing into Western
Europe, though the threat that another embargo will do so
should not be discounted; it did affect the price of oil, no
small matter when OPEC price rises in 1973–74 took away
roughly two percent of West Germany's national income.[9]
Though the likelihood that the OPEC cartel can hold to-
gether has grown more dubious in the light of the Iraqi-
Iranian war, the oil producers—separately or together—will
doubtless continue to push up the price of oil.

To manage to keep the price of oil at a reasonable level
—no higher, say, than the overall level of inflation of the
European Community, the United States and Japan—
would require what international oil consultant Walter J.
Levy calls "an accommodation between oil producers and oil
importers where both parties take full account of each others' vital interests."[10] Specifically, it would mean establishing effective agreements between producers and importers
on the size of exports, the sustainable level of prices, and
planning and implementation of development programs for
the oil-producing countries of the region. This is hardly
likely to happen—not least because it presupposes regional
stability rather than conflict, and a Soviet Union benevo-
lently looking on rather than trying to make its own deals
with the Arabs, through military intimidation if necessary.

Instead, as Levy gloomily predicts, "We will probably be
confronted by a series of major oil crises which might take
any or all of several forms: fighting for control over oil

resources among importing countries or between the super-powers; an economic-financial crisis in importing countries; regional conflicts affecting the oil-producing areas; or internal revolutions or other upheavals in the Middle East. At best, it would appear that a series of future emergencies centering around oil will set back world progress for many, many years . . . with all that this might imply for the political stability of the West, its free institutions, and its internal and external security."[11] The inability—or perhaps, more correctly, unwillingness—of the United States and its allies in Europe and Japan to develop common policies toward the region can only help make Levy's dire predictions come true. For America to be gravely dependent on imported oil only heightens the competition—all the more so when we refuse to conserve oil in order to reduce our dependence in the short term without knowing whether a program to expand domestic production will pay over the long haul, or just how long that will be.

THE GRAVEST danger facing the West today is that what divides us from our allies will prove far greater than what unites us. If Europeans should worry about a more national-istic America, Americans should fear isolating themselves from their allies. To prevent this, we have to be clear on what we want. We can urge our allies to do more for their own defense—and already there are positive signs of grow-ing French-German defense cooperation—but we must continue to be willing to pay the price for their essential security needs. We often tell the Europeans and the Japa-nese that they must ease our burden in defense matters—

and with their strong economies, they should—but these are not burdens we have reluctantly assumed. Nor would we be content if the allies no longer believed in the truth or validity of the American nuclear guarantee and provided wholly for their own defense.

If this happened, German and Japanese power would almost certainly revive—exactly the reverse of our considered policy that Germany and Japan should remain militarily circumscribed. We do not want a remilitarized Western Germany, one that would surely dominate Western Europe —even though France now possesses nuclear weapons—and might be tempted to achieve its dream of unification by force of arms. Nor do we want to see a rearmed Japan (perhaps in alliance with China) seeking primacy in the Pacific. This means that we must pay the principal price for the security of both Germany and Japan. Moreover, we must convince the Europeans and the Japanese that we *can* pay the price—since we do not want their resources denied us, their bases unavailable, their policies possibly in dangerous conflict with our own, and so find ourselves isolated.

The essential requirement for stable strategic deterrence between the United States and the Soviet Union—and thus the guarantee of European and Japanese security—is that the U.S. strategic forces be able to survive a Soviet attack and then be able to respond so effectively that the Russians, knowing this, will not attack in the first place. The effectiveness of the guarantee, as McGeorge Bundy has pointed out, "has not depended on [U.S.] strategic superiority" over the Russians. We have not possessed overwhelming superiority for twenty years. Rather, stable strategic deterrence has rested on two facts: an American military presence in Europe and the Pacific, and the likelihood that, if the Russians attacked, the armed engagement could not be localized, so that a general war would ensue.

From time to time Europeans ask themselves if we will retaliate against the Soviet Union, should the Soviets use nuclear weapons solely against Western Europe. In short, are we willing to risk Chicago for Hamburg? The answer has to be yes—precisely because the defense of Europe is in our interest. Of course, no one can prove that a major attack on Western Europe would escalate to the intercontinental nuclear level. But, as Bundy puts it, "the essential point is the opposite; no one can possibly know it would not."[12] The United States can reassure the allies that the American guarantee will deter an aggressor only so long as we continue to maintain and improve the current position of our strategic and conventional military forces.

None of this means that the United States should prefer its allies weak or cravenly dependent. Far better for the United States to have allies like France and Britain and the Federal Republic of Germany with a strong sense of identity than to be connected to a group of separate but alien states with attendant resentments and confusions. There is, in fact, evidence of growing cooperation between West Germany and France not only in defense but, more significant, in economic matters. A French-German policy brought about the erection of a European monetary system that is supposed to provide a "zone of stability" to counteract the fluctuations of the American economy. As we have noted, an incipient European foreign policy, not always to our liking, has developed toward the Middle East in urging Israel to seek accommodation with the Palestine Liberation Organization. The European Community has concluded special trade arrangements with many developing countries in Africa, the Pacific and the Caribbean. All these independent initiatives demonstrate a growing cohesion in European power and policy, testifying to Europe's desire to return, in French President Giscard d'Estaing's words, "to its power and influence in the world."

Nonetheless, despite these brave words, Europe—or what is now the unwieldy European Community—remains constricted by her inability to rise above her habitual dependence on the United States, what Stanley Hoffmann calls "a cozy belief that the risks and responsibilities of world politics belong to Washington alone, a failure of will and a shrinking of ambition which create a gap . . . between Europe's worldwide concern and its timidity of ambition."[13]

One alternative to a nuclear-armed, remilitarized Europe pursuing policies that could conflict with our own would be the emergence of what many experts in Washington have called "Euro-neutralism." This means, in Walter Laqueur's words, "a new relationship between Europe and the Soviet Union that would amount to undeclared neutralism (rather than, as in the Finnish case, neutrality sanctioned by a treaty)."[14] In either case, the allies will have chosen their role because of their perception of American weakness. In either case, the United States will be isolated.

As yet there is no threat of vengeful German or Japanese power. Nor is there anything so thought-through as Euro-neutralism. Instead, what we should fear is the emergence of a Balkanized Europe—some states returning to utter dependence on the United States, others looking for an accommodation with Moscow, and still others seeking an exclusively national nuclear defense.[15] A fragmenting alliance rather than a European third force—either neutralist or able to fend for itself—would be the most plausible danger confronting the West if we were to pursue a new policy of global containment.

To ensure the integrity of the alliance structure—providing for the bulk of Europe's and Japan's security in order to provide better for our own—it is not enough to be able to maintain military parity with the Soviet Union. It also means controlling our central relationship with the Soviet Union beyond the European and Japanese theaters by devising a strategy for competing with the Soviet Union in the Third World without allowing this competition to drag ourselves and our allies into nuclear war.

In my own discussions with the Soviets, I felt that Seweryn Bialer was right when he described the Soviet Union as an unsatiated power. Trapped by their own belief in Russian power and the ideology of international communism, the Soviets are eager to extend their power into areas which are not, strictly speaking, their or our primary interests. But as they try to get "on the side of change," as they would put it, their intrusion into these areas could indeed threaten our vital interests. Yet while this competition between the superpowers has evident dangers, the United States has to accept it. Despite the rise of regional powers, such as Brazil or India or Nigeria, the Soviets do not see any decline in the determining role that the U.S.-Soviet conflict plays in international politics. Since this attitude so profoundly affects U.S.-Soviet relations, we cannot, much as we might like to, ignore Soviet behavior in the Third World.

As the Soviets see it, the United States is now aware of the difficulty of influencing the Third World through American economic power. For one thing, they believe, as many American experts also do, that we can no longer develop close economic ties with the Third World simply by "recycling" petrodollars through our economy, providing the oil-producing nations with the modern trappings of industrialization—from nuclear power stations to supersonic jets. The volume of petrodollars, they argue, has grown too large for this kind of operation, and the desire of the oil producers for rapid modernization has flagged as the rulers of the Third World witnessed the destabilizing effects of modernization in Iran. Both because of the changed economic situation and the generalized turmoil that exists—as revealed, for example, in the Iraqi-Iranian conflict—they believe that we are now planning to intimidate the Third World through our military forces, as witness our build-up in the Indian Ocean.

Since they assume that we will grow more and more dependent on the Third World for natural resources—not only for Persian Gulf oil but also, for example, for Nigerian oil and Zairean copper—they are convinced that we will engage in new interventions to secure these needs. In their formulation, we are using the idea of a Soviet military threat in the Middle East as "a pretext" so that we can become the regional, if no longer the world, policeman. At the same time, we are willing to let the "Fourth World," that is to say, the poorest nations on this earth, fall by the wayside.

As a result of this analysis, the Soviets are determined not to allow us to exclude them from the Middle East; moreover, because of the turmoil there and elsewhere, and the resentments that our repeated interventions will cause, the Soviet Union believes that it will have new opportunities to expand its influence at our expense.

The main problem for the superpowers, engaged in a competition which, however it arose in the first place, has become in great measure implacable, is to prevent the rivalry from turning into a general conflict and ultimately threatening a nuclear holocaust. In order to do this, the United States will have to concentrate on the central relationship with the Soviet Union. And by now, it consists largely of hostility. Virtually the only positive connection between the superpowers are negotiations over arms control. The economic agreements designed by Nixon and Kissinger in the early 1970s to entangle the Soviet Union and the United States in a web of relationships that would open the door to a widening of détente, including the notion that the superpowers would exercise self-restraint in the Third World, hardly exist.

If we refuse to pursue arms control agreements—both on the overall strategic level of SALT I and SALT II and on the narrower regional plane from the Atlantic to the Urals —then we are abandoning any hope of ending an arms race. For there is no way either side can attain nuclear superiority unless either Washington or Moscow unilaterally abandons its nuclear arsenal and its commitment to strategic parity, an unlikely prospect. As Averell Harriman put it: "It would be . . . folly to assume that better control of nuclear arms can result from a race to nuclear superiority. My reading of the Soviet experience—and I have met with every Soviet leader from Lenin to Brezhnev—indicates that Moscow will sacrifice what it takes to remain equal—as we will, too. The conclusion will not be superiority; the end will be an arms race without end."[16]

It is in the national interest to pursue continuing arms control agreements, the one a precondition to another, since for some time to come such agreements may be the only instruments left to us to contain the ultimate danger of the Soviet-American global competition. Moreover, the process of arms control is vital in shaping our relationship with our allies. We cannot expect Western Europe to maintain an effective continental defense coordinated with our own if we refuse to discuss with the Soviets both the intercontinental strategic arms race and the military balance in the European theater itself.

Despite the troubles that beset them, our alliances are intact precisely because of the threat of Soviet expansion. In this sense, the alliances are there to contain the Soviet Union in Europe and in the northeast Pacific. The economic and military strength of Western Europe acts as a counterweight not only to any direct Soviet thrust across the continent—an unlikely event—but also against Soviet intimidation and against the possibility that the Soviets will take advantage of instability in neutral or nonaligned countries like Austria or Yugoslavia. The Atlantic Alliance is not an alliance dedicated to controlling the internal political evolution of the member-states. Nor should we try to expand it in order to formally coordinate policies outside the geographical area which encompasses it.

Although at times the alliance can work together in dealing with Soviet adventurism in the Third World—and a strengthened European military presence on the continent can more easily allow the use of American troops elsewhere —the American perception of how to deal with Soviet adventurism or expansionism in the Third World may well collide with our allies' views. We need strong alliances as they are, and we should not devote our energies to a constant search for agreements to endorse American behavior outside the Treaty areas. On the other hand, informal meetings on a regular basis to include the United States, Great Britain, France and West Germany—and, when appropriate, Japan —could prove an effective way to cooperate with our allies in coping with crises in the Third World. Indeed, the policies pursued by our allies elsewhere may often be wiser than our own, and we can surely learn from each other. The alliances are not ends in themselves—they are there to contain the expansionism of the Soviet Union. This is not a modest role, after all, and to strengthen our alliances in place is no mean task.

WHAT, IN ESSENCE, are the foreign policy priorities that will help us maintain our alliances and manage the conflict between ourselves and the Soviets so that our rivalry does not lead to nuclear war?

Since foreign policy commitments can finally only be validated by war, the essential condition for our defense is to maintain military forces capable of fulfilling these commitments. Because we are now far more vulnerable in our conventional than in our strategic power, this means, as we have seen, the repair and refurbishing of our conventional forces, including the use of conscription. By reinstituting a conscript army—like the armies fielded by the nations of continental Europe—we can best persuade the Europeans to provide greater support for our combat troops in order to further reduce "the risk factor"—what the military call the gap between our requirements and our capabilities. For as that gap widens—and our reduced reserve strength adds to it—the risk that a conventional war will turn into a nuclear one increases, until we find ourselves in a situation where we must move from a battalion on the ground to an intercontinental nuclear war with little or no flexibility in between.[17]

The nonmilitary arm of an effective foreign policy is foreign aid—whether it be to sustain a NATO ally like Turkey or stabilize a newly revolutionary society like Nicaragua. Foreign assistance is not simply the poor box—though human decency requires us to try to reduce human suffering—but it is a less costly and often more effective way to influence the behavior of other nations, both friend and foe, than intimidation by military force.

Both for economic and strategic reasons, we should move rapidly to cut back or eliminate dependence on foreign resources, and, in particular, to reduce as much as possible the $100 billion annual tax OPEC levies on us in the form of payments for their petroleum. Our unwillingness to do this weakens us in the eyes of our allies and adversaries every bit as much as does our reluctance to impose conscription or appropriate a few million dollars to help ensure stability in our own backyard.[18]

Not least, arms control agreements with the Soviets should not be thought of as the road back to détente, and, even less, as a reward for good behavior. Nor should they be left to the Europeans to pursue while we embark on an arms race. Rather, they should be used as a way to restrain the arms race until such time as the political climate changes so that both superpowers find themselves in a more cooperative, less confrontational posture. Diplomacy is not the enemy of military force unless a nation's foreign policy is uncertain, vacillating, and, finally, self-destructive.

None of these things can be done effectively, however, if we go on financing the defense of America's vital interests on credit, producing less than the total of what we consume and expend on defense. We will then surely end up by being unable to protect those very interests we are committed to defend. From tariffs to interest rates, competition rather than cooperation will come to dominate the alliance. It will become an unnatural alliance—if it exists at all.

In the fall of 1979, Chancellor Helmut Schmidt speculated on the possible decline of the West, and his warnings were surely directed at the United States as much as at Western Europe. He said: "The oil producers' cartel is nowadays as great a menace to the functioning of the world's economy as is the menace of governments going it the easy way by printing more money and parliaments asking for more spending and less revenue. This is the way by which you ruin empires, states, world powers."[19] European leaders such as Schmidt and Giscard d'Estaing are, in varying degrees, frustrated by America's unwillingness to defend her vital foreign interests by adjusting her domestic priorities. Unless we do so, we will finally be unable to maintain the confidence of our allies and the integrity of our alliances.

Nor can we place the blame on others—not on the Soviets, not on the Arab oil producers—if we remain unwilling to pay for the defense of our vital interests because we have mismanaged our economy. Outside forces reap the benefits of our wanton behavior; they do not cause it. As Henry Kaufman, in analyzing our inability to control inflation, points out, the enemy is ourselves. We cannot fault government or central bankers or some other abstract force for throwing us into disarray. After all, as Kaufman says, "we live in a democratic political system and no government leading such a system can long be independent in will and action of the electorate from which it ultimately must derive its power. Our government reflects, admittedly with a time lag, our individual strengths and weaknesses, our aspirations and our morality. There are no moats around Washington and our state and local governments from which edicts are hurled at us."[20]

What "we" do reflects itself in the society we have created, a society that today is not ready to mobilize itself to cope with the economic crisis. The danger when the economy no longer provides underlying stability for its citizens is disorder leading to chaos and, further, to authoritarianism, a possibility even for the United States. Such a grave threat, as Robert Heilbroner has eloquently put it, would come from a quickening of our present double-digit inflation up to the "Latin American" levels of 50 to 150 percent a year, or, the ultimate horror, the wild inflation of Weimar Germany, which also began with an attempt to pay foreign debts with a devalued currency. The logic of inflation suggests that such a progression might occur since "inflation feeds upon itself." When we expect prices to rise by, say, ten percent, we ask for more money, say, 15 percent, to get ahead of the anticipated increase. If everyone succeeds at this and inflation itself is at a 15-percent level, our "income objectives" rise accordingly to 20 percent. Thus, "what began as an orderly rush becomes a wild rush, as everyone tries to move up to the first rank."[21]

Unfortunately the crisis in our domestic economy and social policy, so interconnected with our foreign policy, is still masked by the enormity of our power. We have all the trappings of a great nation. If our power is proportionately less than it was twenty years ago, we are hardly reduced to our own shores. If the Soviets choose to engage us in a competition for power or influence in the Third World, it is a competition that they are not predestined to win. The alliances we have built up still hedge in the Soviet Union in the East and West. Our technology and our culture are everywhere sought out—by the Soviet Union not least of all, for the United States is, as a rich society, what the Soviet Union wants to be. But the dangers of America's decline, as we have seen, are already evident—with continuing trade deficits as we spend ourselves into insolvency, and as we refuse to consume less and produce more until our capital is exhausted and with it the world we have known.

There is a limit to how long a great nation can allow itself to be governed by those who lack the capacity to lead. For a time its failures can be covered up—a trade deficit can be compensated for by an influx of foreign capital leading to an overall balance-of-payments surplus; its alliances appear to be intact until they are tested; its standing army may be large yet badly maintained with inadequate reserves. The danger is that when the crisis can no longer be hidden there will be no providential statesman to reinvigorate a society in peril.

This is what Felix Rohatyn believes. In his view, it may already be too late to expect politicians to cope with the crisis that is upon us. Instead, despite the danger to the democratic process, the road back to statesmanship may require us to rely more and more on appointed boards to manage our affairs. Rohatyn proposes that the executive call for a Temporary National Economic Committee, modeled after F.D.R.'s 1938 body of the same name, to recommend an integrated domestic and international economic strategy for the next two years. He makes a compelling argument for such a commission for two basic reasons: "First, because nowhere in government today does strategic economic planning take place; second, because difficult, controversial policies must originate from non-political, credible bodies, created in an atmosphere of emergency, to generate the political support enabling the President and the Congress to act."[22]

With the election of Ronald Reagan, a quite different path from what Rohatyn suggests has been chosen, one of less rather than more government direction. A great debate may be in the offing. If so, it is one with the highest stakes —for this society is unlikely to hold together if we do not achieve an economy that allows for consumption without profligacy. Beneath the society in crisis is the Hobbesian underworld where dog will eat dog.

Whatever the outcome, the threat to the national interest is real and immediate. Dynamic leadership in a democracy too often comes only at the last moment—if, indeed, it comes at all: de Gaulle did not lead France in June of 1940 and Churchill did not lead Britain in September 1939. For as de Gaulle wisely wrote many decades before he returned to power in 1958 to restore France's political and economic strength, "A statesman may be determined and tenacious, may have the backing of all the resources of a great country and a solid system of alliances, but, if he does not understand the character of his time, he will fail."[23]

Is it too late to find statesmen capable of succeeding? It soon will be unless we discern in our leaders an essential understanding of the character of our time—that we are caught in a conflict between the ideals of a consumer society, which are the expectations of an ever-higher standard of living, and the hollowness of those ideals if they are not supported by a secure and solvent nation. Consumption even in a consumer society can only be a secondary goal; the first goal is to preserve the integrity of the society, which means we have to be able to afford what we want. If we continue to construct a society on the windy scaffolding of credit, that society will not be able to withstand a threat from without. Until we acknowledge this, no public consensus can possibly emerge on the measures needed for a valid foreign policy.

It has been clear for some time now that the American political leadership either does not understand the nature of our vital interests or cannot effectively mobilize public opinion to defend them. Unlike Great Britain in the nineteenth century—from Pitt and Castlereagh at the beginning to Salisbury at the end—America after Vietnam has lost a sense of balance in her foreign policy. We do not seem able to distinguish between our primary and our secondary interests. We do not seem able to connect our profligacy at home with our weakness abroad.

The overextension of American power came to an end with Vietnam. We should not seek to enlarge our power by increasing our commitments any more than we should look for new ways to shed our existing ones. As it is, we are hard put to maintain enough military strength to defend Western Europe and the Western Pacific. We continue to remain gravely dependent on imported oil, which circumscribes our actions in the Persian Gulf. An anti-Soviet consensus leading to a new crusade of global containment will not only strain our resources to such a degree that we will have to live with an enormous military establishment and a continuing reduction in our standard of living, but will also stretch our alliances to the breaking point. In such a world we will face both a Balkanization of Europe and a fierce competition for Middle Eastern oil, with the Soviet Union dealt into the game.

Isolated within an increasingly anarchic world, we will have lost much of our present ability to defend our vital interests as they are, and the exercise of our power, far-flung across the globe, will be gradually reduced. On the other hand, should we show ourselves able to regain our economic strength and use it to defend our alliances, we would also redeem our prestige in international affairs—a prestige which is the recognition by others of our power. In foreign relations as in domestic affairs, the way to restore the balance between our commitments and our power is to increase our means and, in this way, to regain our lost solvency. For if we remain insolvent, how can we have a foreign policy at all?

Notes

I

1 "vast machine": Samuel Dill, *Roman Society in the Last Century of the Western Empire*, 2nd ed., 1899, reprint ed., Cleveland: World Publishing Company, Meridian Books, 1958, p. 229. See also David Fromkin, *The Question of Government*, New York: Scribner's, 1975, pp. 44–45.

2 Earl Ravenal, "The Nixon Doctrine and our Asian Commitments," *Foreign Affairs*, January 1971, p. 201.

3 Quote from an address by Felix G. Rohatyn for the French-American Chamber of Commerce, New York, December 1, 1978.

4 From "Growth in productivity" . . . to "manage her economy," see *The Economist*, London, 27 January–2 February 1979, pp. 11–12.

5 See Seweryn Bialer, *Stalin's Successors*, New York: Cambridge University Press, 1980, p. 2. See also Seweryn Bialer, "A Risk Carefully Taken," *The Washington Post*, January 18, 1980, op-ed page.

6 Richard Stebbins, *The United States in World Affairs, 1954*, New York: Harper and Brothers, 1956, p. 181.

7 See David P. Calleo and Benjamin M. Rowland, *America and the World Political Economy*, Bloomington: Indiana University Press, 1973 (paper), p. 3.

8 *Ibid.*, pp. 44–45.

9 David Calleo, *The Atlantic Fantasy*, Baltimore: The Johns Hopkins University Press, 1970 (paper), pp. 84–85.

10 David Calleo, "American Foreign Economic Policy in the Sixties," chapter 2: "The Kennedy Years (1961–1963)," from a draft chapter presented at The Lehrman Institute, April 11, 1979, p. 9, from his forthcoming book *The Imperious Economy: U.S. Policy at Home and Abroad, 1960–1980.*

11 *Ibid.*

12 *Ibid.*, p. 10.

13 *Ibid.*, p. 17.

14 See Calleo, *The Atlantic Fantasy*, p. 84.

15 See *Hearings Before the Committee on Foreign Relations, U.S. Senate*, "Impact of the War in Southeast Asia on the Economy," Part I, April 15 and 16, 1970, U.S. Government Printing Office, Washington, D.C., pp. 67–68.

16 See Calleo, draft chapter, The Lehrman Institute, April 11, 1979, p. 25.

17 *Ibid.*, p. 37.

18 *U.S. Senate Hearings, op. cit.*, p. 30.

19 "In terms of economic efficiency . . . Algeria is the undisputed leader," Alistair Horne, *A Savage War of Peace*, New York: The Viking Press, 1977, p. 558.

20 "It was in Algeria . . . the Arab-Israeli War the following month," *Ibid.*, p. 559.

21 See Laurence Scheinman, *Atomic Energy Policy in France Under the Fourth Republic*, Princeton: Princeton University Press, 1965, p. xxi.

22 "it would not be an overstatement . . . against her enemies," *Ibid.*, p. xxii.

11

1 See *The Federalist*, New York: New American Library, Master Edition: Jay, No. 2; Hamilton, No. 6; Madison, No. 10.

For Washington quote, Hans Morgenthau, *Politics Among Nations*, New York: Knopf, 4th Edition, 1967, p. 8.

2 See Harold van Buren Cleveland, "Inflation and the Politicization of Economic Life," from *Theology and Culture*, Essays in honor of Albert T. Mollegen and Clifford Stanley, ed. New York: W. Stevenson, Anglican Theological Review, 1977.

3 See *The Wall Street Journal*, June 3, 1980.

4 See Robert Legvold, "Containment Without Confrontation," *Foreign Policy*, Fall 1980, p. 94.

5 See *Strategic Survey*, 1979, London: IISS, p. 10.

6 See C.W. Maynes and Richard Ullman, "Ten Years of Foreign Policy," *Foreign Policy*, Fall 1980, p. 6.

7 *Ibid.*

8 See *The Washington Post*, January 28, 1980.

9 See Henry Kaufman, "The Disregard for Capital," Salomon Brothers report, May 1, 1980, p. 2. See also Jason Epstein, "Friendly Fascism," *The New York Review of Books*, October 23, 1980, p. 14.

10 See David Calleo's "Ford's Recovery," a draft chapter presented at The Lehrman Institute, January 30, 1980, pp. 7–8, from his forthcoming book *The Imperious Economy: U.S. Policy at Home and Abroad, 1960–1980*.

11 See *The Washington Post*, January 22, 1980. See also Robert Stobaugh and Daniel Yergin, "Energy: An Emergency Telescoped," *Foreign Affairs*, "America and the World 1979."

12 Monthly Energy Review, U.S. Department of Energy, February 1980.

13 According to John Sawhill, Testimony before Senate Foreign Relations Committee, February 20, 1980, 31 percent of total U.S. petroleum imports came from the Persian Gulf.

14 *The Wall Street Journal,* March 30, 1980, p. 31.

15 The Federal Reserve Bank of New York's *Quarterly Review,* Winter, 1979/80, p. 24.

16 Economic Report of the President, January 1980, p. 85, *O.E.C.D.* data; in *The Wall Street Journal,* February 29, 1980.

17 FRBNY, *op. cit.,* p. 28.

18 John Volpe, "Technological Change as a Determinant of U.S. Competitiveness," *Assessing U.S. Competitiveness in World Markets,* Washington: International Division, Chamber of Commerce of the United States, 1979, p. 8.

19 *Ibid.,* p. 11. See also *Science and Technology: Promises and Dangers in the Eighties.* President's Commission for a National Agenda for the Eighties. Report of the Panel on Science and Technology, Promises and Dangers (U.S. Government Printing Office, 1980), pp. 22–27.

20 See *The Economist* (London), "Japan Survey," February 1980, pp. 23–29 See also Felix Rohatyn, "Reconstructing America," *The New York Review of Books,* March 5, 1981.

21 See *The New York Times,* January 16, 1981; *The Washington Post,* January 16, 1981; *Newsweek,* January 19, 1981.

22 See *Business Week.* January 21, 1980, p. 84.

23 See *Business Week,* February 4, 1980, p. 80.

24 *Ibid.,* p. 81; See also Stanley Karnow, "The Hidden Costs of the Carter Doctrine," *Baltimore Sun,* February 4, 1980, p. 12.

25 Robert W. Tucker, "America in Decline: The Foreign

Policy of Maturity," *Foreign Affairs*, "America and the World 1979," pp. 476–477. See also *The Wall Street Journal*, "Hard Choices on Defense Spending," January 21, 1981.

26 See Herbert Scoville, "America's Greatest Construction: Can It Work?" *The New York Review of Books*, March 20, 1980. See also Sidney Drell, "Sum," *Arms Control Today*, September 1979.

27 See James Fallows, "Muscle-Bound Superpower," *The Atlantic*, October 1979. See also the Boston Study Group, *The Price of Defense* New York: Times Books, 1979.

28 See Adam Yarmolinsky, "Military Balance: About Equal," *The New York Times*, February 4, 1980. The figures on numbers of nuclear warheads came from the *NYT*, September 21, 1980, p. 58.

29 See Barry R. Posen and Stephen W. Van Evera, "Overarming and Underwhelming," *Foreign Policy*, Fall 1980, pp. 100–101.

30 Quoted in *The New York Times*, September 9, 1980, p. A1.

31 See Subrata N. Chakravaty, "The Great Push-Button Delusion," *Forbes*, September 15, 1980, pp. 49–61.

32 See William Hauser, "A Hollow Army?", *Foreign Affairs*, Spring 1981.

33 All quotes from Walter Lippmann are from his book, *U.S. Foreign Policy: Shield of the Republic*, Boston: Atlantic-Little Brown, 1943.

III

1 See Robert W. Tucker, "The Purposes of American Power," *Foreign Affairs*, Winter 1980/81, pp. 266–268.

2 See *The New York Times*, November 13, 1980, p. A8.

3 See David Watt, *The Economist,* October 11, 1980, pp. 19–20.

4 *The Economist,* November 8, 1980, "West German Economy Survey," p. 20. See also *The Wall Street Journal*, December 15, 1980.

5 *The New York Times,* November 15, 1980, p. A1.

6 See Giovanni Agnelli, "East-West Trade: A European View," *Foreign Affairs,* Summer 1980, p. 1022; see also *Time,* December 1, 1980.

7 See *The Wall Street Journal,* November 19, 1980.

8 See David Watt, "The Atlantic Alliance," *The Economist,* October 11, 1980.

9 See "West German Economy Survey," *The Economist,* November 8, 1980, p. 5.

10 See Walter J. Levy, "Oil and the Decline of the West," *Foreign Affairs,* Summer 1980, p. 1014.

11 *Ibid.,* p. 1015.

12 For a clear analysis of this problem, see McGeorge Bundy, "Strategic Deterrence After Thirty Years—What Has Changed?," Remarks made at the Annual Conference, IISS, Villars, Switzerland, September 7, 1979, published in *Survival* (London), November/December 1979.

13 Stanley Hoffmann, "The Crisis in the West," *The New York Review of Books,* July 17, 1980.

14 See Walter Laqueur, "Euro-Neutralism," *Commentary,* June 1980.

15 See Pierre Lellouche, "La Sécurité de l'Europe dans les Années 80: Essai de Synthèse et de Prospective," Programme de Recherche sur "Les Dimensions de la Sécurité de l'Europe," IFRI, Paris, October 1980, p. 69.

16 W. Averell Harriman, "SALT II—Unfinished Business," *The New York Times,* October 25, 1980.

17 See William Hauser, *op. cit.*

18 See also Felix Rohatyn, "The Coming Emergency and What Can Be Done About It," *The New York Review of Books,* December 4, 1980.

19 Interview with Helmut Schmidt, *The Economist,* September 29, 1979.

20 See Henry Kaufman, *op. cit.*, p. 6.

21 See Robert Heilbroner, "The Inflation in Your Future," *The New York Review of Books,* May 1, 1980, pp. 9–10.

22 Felix G. Rohatyn, Address to the 1980 Financial Conference of the Conference Board, New York City, February 28, 1980.

23 Charles de Gaulle, "The Edge of the Sword," New York: Criterion Books, 1960, p. 80 (originally published in French as *Le Fil de l'Epée,* 1932).

JAMES CHACE is managing editor of *Foreign Affairs.* The author and editor of four previous books and more than forty major articles on foreign policy, he has traveled extensively in Eastern and Western Europe, the Soviet Union and Latin America. He has taught at Yale, Columbia and Georgetown universities. Mr. Chace lives with his family in New York City.